THE CHURCH UNDER
THE CROSS

by

J. B. PHILLIPS

New York - 1956

THE MACMILLAN COMPANY

First Printing

Printed in the United States of America

Library of Congress catalog card number: 56–10964

PREFACE TO THE AMERICAN EDITION

IT WILL be obvious to all who read the following pages that this is a book written by a Church of England clergyman on the work of The Church Missionary Society, a Society originally founded within the Church of England in 1799. To have such a book accepted for publication in the United States is to me a heart-warming experience, partly because it serves to remind me of the unfailing courtesy, kindliness and generosity which I experienced during my visit to the United States in 1954, and partly because the very act of acceptance by publishers such as The Macmillan Company shows that American Christians of many denominations may be expected to read about what is in effect a "global" situation, written about by one English Episcopalian.

It might not be out of place here to mention that what finally drew me to your great country was not natural curiosity (though I have plenty of that), nor the kindly appreciative letters (though I have plenty of those), but the personal visits of several groups of young Christians who came to see me on their way to or from the Work-camps and Rehabilitation Centers of stricken post-war Europe. I felt I was meeting not merely fine warm-hearted youngsters ready to donate part of their vacation for the good of others, but living representatives of a new spirit rising in the Church. Here was no narrow vision, no parochial enthusiasm, no boasting of a local Church's achievements, but a real concern for the whole scattered and broken family of God. I was very deeply moved by meeting year after year young people with such a vision of God's world-wide Purpose. In the end I felt compelled to visit the country and some of the Churches which had produced such cheerful willingness to serve under the Cross.

I am confident from what I saw and heard during those five short weeks in your country that there are many who will not only sympathise with the purpose of this book, but who will also be one with me in seeing beyond denominational barriers and in humbly attempting to follow the vast patient Purpose of God. We are all together in this tremendous struggle against fear, superstition and sin. My hope and my prayer is that the readers of this book will realise afresh why there is of necessity a Cross in every Christian life, and how there can be no true piece of Christian service without its own particular Cross. Obviously the scope of this book is limited, but what things in it are eternally true and useful will, I am certain, be echoed and endorsed by many generous and vigorous American churches.

Because the needs of the front-line troops are always so great, and because the men and women who man the outposts of the Kingdom of Christ are often loth to advertise what they are doing, I should like it to be known that I, who am a writer by vocation, and not one of the front-line troops, have written this book as a small act of appreciation of what such unsung heroes and heroines are doing under the Cross. And it is my privilege to give the whole of the proceeds on the sale of this book to help forward the world-wide work of The Church Missionary Society.

J. B. Phillips

Swanage, 1956.

CONTENTS

AUTHOR'S FOREWORD

I CONSIDER it a high honor and privilege to be asked to write this book for the Church Missionary Society. But I should like to make it plain from the outset that, although the Society has provided me with the information, it is in no way responsible for the views expressed in the following pages, for they are entirely my own.

May I begin by remarking upon the happy coincidence, or possibly the Providence of God, that has led me to write this book almost as soon as I had completed the translation of The Acts of the Apostles? For there is a strong similarity in feel and atmosphere between the Young Church in Action (the title I gave to my translation) and today's Church, which of course includes many young Churches, in action in our day and generation.

It seems to me that many people scarcely appreciate the miracle of the Young Church—that here, for the first time in human history, was a small band of human beings commissioned by God Himself to change the world! I have written elsewhere of the drive, the resilience and the gay courage of that unconquerable fellowship which began to turn the world upside down within the span of a man's lifetime. The feel of it all, the joyful discovery that God's plan was beginning to work, the equally joyful acceptance of humiliation and suffering for the sake of the much-loved Name, have left with me what is, I hope, an indelible impression. I am sure I shall not easily forget St. Luke's artless but vivid story of men and women wide open to the Spirit of God. With divine appropriateness that Spirit comes upon the scene with the sound of a boisterous gale and the sign of blazing fire. That celestial wind never drops and that holy fire never dies down as we see the Young Church going forward, vulnerable, fearless, flexible and splendid, to carry love and light into a world darkened by hatred and fear.

It is with the same lifting of the heart and with the same sense of "God at work" that I read letters and reports from overseas. Here, instead of a petty-minded parochialism or the stuffiness of an ingrowing churchiness, I can breathe the fresh air, the air in which there is the unmistakable tang of the moving Spirit of God. Of course, these records reveal no mere catalogue of triumphs. There are setbacks and disappointments, difficulties and even disasters enough to make the angels weep. But—to my mind at least—among this far-flung scattered army of the men and women of Christ there flourish the same gay courage, the same unconquerable loyalty as I found in the history of the Young Church. There are places in this world where the Church has grown fat and complacent; there are places where the spiritual equivalent of middle-aged spread or finicky old age are only too apparent. But for the secret of youth commend me to the missionary enterprises and the Younger Churches! The very toughness and complexity of the situations, the very fact that the emissaries of the Most High are in daily contact with the overt forces of evil, call for an athleticism of spirit which ensures the perpetual youthfulness of the missionary Church. Nineteen hundred years have passed since St. Luke wrote the Acts, but as I read of what is happening today I feel I am still reading of the Young Church in action.

I have never been a missionary myself, though that was long my heart's desire, but I grasp with both hands the opportunity of paying tribute to this magnificent, unadvertised army. I know many missionaries personally, and at summer schools and elsewhere I have met many more. I believe there is no body of people who more deserve our respect, our admiration and our support. It should not be a spiritual chore but a high privilege to support these front-line warriors with our prayers. I confess that I am often outraged by the world's treatment of such committed, dedicated lives. Nothing is more easy than for a novelist or playwright to jeer at the "simple" missionary, or to build his own success upon the theme of a lonely missionary who "goes wrong." I grow very weary of disparaging remarks about missionaries made by men who are not fit to black their boots.

Now I would challenge all those who sit comfortably at home and disparage the work of the missionaries and jeer at "native Christians." What have they ever done to win a single person from darkness to light? Have they read, since they were grown-up people, the New Testament, which perhaps they knew patchily as children? Can they explain the fact that in the same New Testament people are changed in the very citadel of their being; cowards become heroes, thieves become honest men, and those who have been debased by drink or sex stand up and live as sons of God? Does our modern critic have the slightest knowledge that the same miracles of personality-change are taking place today? Has he ever bothered to read the first-hand reports of any missionary, or even the contents of a missionary magazine?

Again, I must remind you that I am expressing purely personal views when I say that to me there is a much more frightening ignorance in our modern world than the "ignorance of the heathen." I am referring to the almost total ignorance of the content and implication of the Christian Faith shown by many "clever" people today. Frankly, I find it horrifying to discover that men who are experts in their own line, in astronomy, genetics, or nuclear physics, for example, have no adult knowledge of what the Church of Christ stands for, and a complete blank ignorance of what the Church is achieving today. It is the more horrifying because people who rightly respect the expert for his knowledge in his own field have no idea that he has not carefully examined and reluctantly discarded Christianity, but in all probability has never studied it at all!

I am more and more convinced that if we could see this world from the angels' point of view a great deal of human activity would appear completely valueless. I doubt if the angels are much interested in the possibility of coloured television or in the breaking of speed records by land, sea and air. In fact, I should not be surprised to learn that, from the celestial viewpoint, the vast bulk of what is regarded as "news" is of very little interest. This would not be because angels dislike human beings or are not interested in the human scene, but simply because so little of what is considered "important" is really relevant to the whole vast battle between light and darkness that is being fought out upon our little planet. If a Fleet Street journalist could see into an angel's mind (and what a help, one can't help thinking, that would be all round!), he would see what appears to him an almost one-track concentration—the angel's news sense would appear to be startlingly narrow. The building of the Kingdom of God, a slow, painful and difficult process, the age-long battle with ignorance, fear, superstition and disease, such things would seem to be of paramount importance. To the astonished journalist the very things with which he normally fills his paper would be seen to be at most of ephemeral value, while the far-off conflicts with evil and ignorance fought out in the unreported, unadvertised fields of human activity would be shown to be front-page news.

There is something else which I feel needs to be said. It is an extraordinary commentary on the present human situation that so many of our finest intellects and most gifted personalities can be plainly seen by the angels to be intentionally or unintentionally avoiding the real issue. Surely the true challenge to humanity is not so much to achieve physical marvels as to change people, and through them to change situations. It is probably part of the moral infection of this planet which makes so many men and women reluctant to cope with problems of personality, to deal with the messy and unpleasant, to join with the awe-full, frightening, patient task of "making men whole." It surely must, in the eyes of the angels, appear to be human escapism of the most lamentable kind when they see intelligent human beings solemnly discussing such projects as visiting the moon, or interplanetary travel, while they do not attempt to cope with a thousand human ills which cry to heaven for the loving service of fellow men.

However, it is no use wringing our hands or expending our energies bewailing what is undoubtedly a wastage of human power and personality. Unless a man is spiritually quickened he quite literally cannot see the Kingdom of God, and he will pour out his energies upon the heroic, the interesting, the profitable or the glamorous, as his own background and temperament suggest. In this book I am concerned with those who are aware of God's vast Plan, and committed to cooperate with it. It has been my privilege to read a great many letters and reports from men and women who are cheerfully and uncomplainingly living their lives under the direction of the Spirit. Here are some of the real builders of history, the true history of this planet. The results and effects of their labors are not merely recorded in heaven; one day they will be plainly demonstrable there, long after all that fills our headlines today has been forgotten like a distant dream.

These outriders of the King, these pioneers of the new humanity, these ambassadors of Christ often work in isolation and obscurity. The true glory and worth of what they do is not yet revealed, and the sign in which they conquer is the sign of sacrifice, the sign of the Cross.

For as the Church has moved forward it has been inescapably THE CHURCH UNDER THE CROSS. Wherever we read reliable Church history, whether of a thousand years ago or of today, whether in this country or in the far-off places of the earth, the same patterns of the Cross repeat themselves. They are quite simply the patterns of human life lived under the direction of the Holy Spirit.

The world is full of people with bright ideas and clever solutions, but the moment these ideas and solutions are geared into actual human situations one aspect or another of the Cross inevitably appears. Although, as we shall see later, there is unique joy and satisfaction of spirit in cooperation with the Mind and Purpose of God Himself, there is no such thing as "Christianity without tears." Until the final curtain falls, the Church, or the individuals who compose the Church, make no real progress unless they live under the Cross.

I

The Preaching of the Cross

To THOSE who are outside the pale of the Church of God (though never, of course, outside the reach of His loving Purpose), there often seems something pathetic and even ridiculous in the Christian's proclaiming of the Cross. St. Paul found his preaching of Christ crucified "foolishness to the Greeks" and "a stumbling-block to the Jews." All his successors find precisely the same thing today. Clever people, the equivalent of the "Greeks" of St. Paul's day, can conceive a Power and a Mind behind all the observed phenomena of life. But it seems to them a stupid approach altogether to present the Supreme Power not only reduced to human stature but dying a criminal's death. For much the same reason, to the "Jews," who represent all those who have the deepest possible reverence for the awe-full majesty of the Most High God (and that today would include the vast hosts of Islam), it is unthinkable that God Himself should suffer not only the degradation of taking human flesh but also the unspeakable humiliation of suffering for mankind as Representative Man. Nevertheless, in a strange, unearthly way the preaching of Christ crucified accomplishes what all the high thinking and clever talk could never do—it changes people.

God's great Act of Reconciliation accomplished through Christ is of cosmic significance, and we should be rash to set any limit to its effect. As John pointed out, Christ "is the propitiation for our sins: and not for ours only, but also for the sins of the whole world" (I John 2. 2). Yet when this tremendous Act dawns significantly upon the individual heart and mind, the effect is intensely personal. St. Paul himself, who was centuries ahead of his time in his sense of the vast, variegated human family whom God willed to reconcile in Christ, could yet speak intimately of Christ's action on the Cross. "Who loved me and gave Himself for me," he records with moving simplicity. Millions since St. Paul's day have found forgiveness, freedom and confidence in God in accepting personally a reconciliation that they themselves were powerless to make.

There is another side to the preaching of Christ crucified. There is much in life which appears to deny a God of Love; and, to be brutally truthful, there is much to make men resentful of a Supreme Power who sits, as it were, in celestial comfort in the heavens, serene and insulated from the world's sin and suffering. Men may indeed feel afraid of such a Being; they may seek His favor or attempt to mollify His anger, but they do not love Him. But when they see that the immeasurable love of God expressed itself by a Personal Visit, by a Personal Redemption, their whole idea of "God" is radically altered. When a man sees to what lengths his God will go to bring him to Himself, the springs of love are not infrequently unsealed.

It is noteworthy in the preaching of the Young Church

in the Acts of the Apostles that the Resurrection appears
to take precedence even over the Cross. It is not, I imagine,
that the Apostles for one moment failed to see the significance of the great Act of Redemption, but that their hearts
were filled to overflowing with the triumph of the Resurrection. Not only was the reconciliation accomplished and endorsed, not only was death plainly a conquered foe, not only
was Christ Himself living, contemporary and present in all
their activities, but the tremendous power which turned that
apparent defeat into resplendent victory was available to
transform and irradiate the personalities of sinful men. St.
Paul once declared it as his ambition to "know him, and
the power of his resurrection, and the fellowship of his sufferings" (*Philippians* 3. 10). I am convinced from my study of
St. Paul's work and writing that he did not merely wish to
experience for himself the enormous power which raised
Christ from the dead, but to see that same power operative
in the lives of hundreds of others. It is perfectly true that
to see something of the significance of the Cross can change
a man's whole outlook; but that is no more than a beginning.
If he is to grow and develop, if he is to move on from peni-
tence and a reversal of all his previous values, and move
forward confidently as a son of God, he needs the power of
the Resurrection.

The mysterious effect upon human personality of the
preaching of the Cross and the subsequent power of the
Resurrection can be illustrated from any of the letters and
reports which lie before me at this moment. Let me take a
few, and may I remind you that this is contemporary history
—this sort of thing is happening almost all over the world.
From East Africa a report reads:

"Never in the previous years of our ministry have we been more conscious that the preaching of the Cross is the power of God unto salvation . . . power to have victory over dishonesty, drunkenness, witchcraft and immorality. Meeting with men and women who have been born again through the power of the preaching of the Cross renews our strength and makes us eager to see what miracle God will do next."

From Egypt comes a report of an Armenian pastor who is being greatly used by God as an evangelist. He is a poor man with a simple message, and his whole method of work is as different as possible from that of the highly organized campaigns which we have lately witnessed and perhaps taken part in. Yet the power of the preaching of the Cross "comes through" with very great effect, and souls are "added to the Lord" as they were in the early Church.

Most of us must have felt bored at one time or another with the apparent verbosity and repetition of the Athanasian Creed. Who could ever guess that the Message of the Cross would burst forth from such a forbidding piece of theological writing? Yet from Uganda we read of a hospital orderly who suddenly exclaimed: "I have been reading the Athanasian Creed and I suddenly saw that God really was in Christ on the Cross reconciling us to Himself by the shed blood."

Again and again missionaries themselves testify to the fact that they need to come back to the Cross and understand afresh the meaning of humility and of self-giving. Prides and prejudices whose existence in their own hearts they had hardly suspected had been stimulated by local frictions. Where else could they find the love that dissolves pride and the inspiration to serve in humility but from the Cross of Christ? As one writer says, "I feel it is only from such a position of

4

one sinner to another, knowing something of the grace of the Lord Jesus, that there is any hope of portraying the meaning of the Cross." Another writes:

"I feel that we missionaries can help more by letting the other Christians see that we too are redeemed sinners, that is the foundation of our fellowship in Him. Yet, looking back on the past four years, I can name only one individual who gives a clear testimony. . . . We all, African, Copt and English, need Him."

From the tiny Church in faraway Japan the same Message is producing the same results in human life. Before me is a report of a nominal Christian who after many years of going to Sunday school as a child has at last seen the point of Christianity, and has been baptized with the sign of the Cross. Another Japanese who is a street preacher is filled with the love of God and the desire to serve his fellow men. He wants no honor for himself; indeed, he wishes to go into the very worst slums to tell of the love of God and of salvation through Christ. "I don't mind if it kills me," he says simply. Where did he learn to express such self-giving love, and where did he find a message for the most debased, except at the foot of the Cross?

Also from Japan there come wonderful reports of real conversions taking place among what we should call the "bad hats" in prison. There is space to quote only briefly:

"One man said he had been a hopeless wastrel all his life. This was his fourth time in prison, and he had caused infinite trouble and anxiety to his family and the authorities. He just did not care and he had no use for religion. Then one day he was persuaded by a cell-mate, one of the Christians, to go to church (as they call my Bible class). He continued to come and after seeing the change baptism had made in his fellow-prisoner, he earnestly sought and came to know Christ as his Saviour. He said he now felt a new man. And a police guard spoke up and said: 'That's perfectly true; he was one of the worst. I've never seen such a change in a man.'"

I quote again from an East African letter, but this particular point is made in many fields:

"A truly converted student does begin to show that 'enlightened understanding.' . . . This side of the matter, this fact that conversion affects the mental capabilities of men who are willing to pray for the Spirit's help should, I feel, never be lost sight of."

Now here is a very remarkable thing: an experienced, intelligent observer has noticed that the reception of the Message of the Cross not only redirects a man's loyalty but actually stimulates his intelligence. I wonder how the enemies of the Christian faith explain this observed phenomenon.

Just as we at home can observe the different working of the same Spirit following the preaching and appreciation of the Message of the Cross, so in the wider field of the Church overseas we can see people being changed by the Message, but not all in the same way or at the same speed. For example, we have all heard or read something of the Revival Movement in Africa, which, whatever its shortcomings, has produced some magnificently devoted Christians; but God is quietly at work where there is no great emotional pressure, as there is bound to be in a revival movement. We read in a letter from the southern Sudan:

"That the Lord is at work there is no doubt, and whilst there is no revival blessing there is the quiet and just as effective working of the Spirit in many a heart."

6

I do not think that there is any implied criticism here of revivalist methods and results. It is quite plain to me, who have had the privilege of reading reports from various places overseas where the Young Church is growing, that what is the right pattern of operation in one area might be quite unnatural and wholly inappropriate in another. The important thing is that men and women are being truly converted to faith in Christ. Here is a simple, almost naïve, but delightful example of how the truth of the new birth in Christ dawned upon a young Nigerian:

"One student (learning geography) called out in class, 'Oh, I see then we are really living on a ball floating in space, and we still do not fall off.' This remark was the turning point for him. All he had learned for a term and a half about the world, its origins, the atmosphere and its marvels became alive, true, illuminated. Three days later in an S.C.M. group discussing 'being born from above' he burst in to explain that it was like his own experience in geography class. 'It just happens and you know it is all true.' "

The strange power of the preaching of the Cross is evident too in the dark and difficult places, where evil has been heavily entrenched for centuries. I wonder what our modern "clevers" would have to say in the face of reports such as these made on the spot by eyewitnesses? Both these extracts are from Kenya letters:

"This has been a wonderfully encouraging year here in many ways. For years this has been one of the hard, dark spots in Kenya, but now here and there little groups of keen Christians are to be found witnessing to the light of the Gospel and the saving power of the Lord Jesus. Some members of these groups are revived Christians and some are people who have come straight from heathenism and have never attended church classes. Together they are finding peace and joy in their new-found fellowship of Christ's Church which is His Body."

"Recently two local witch doctors have been saved and have given up their evil practices. How wonderful is the change in their lives."

That there is something here at work, something immensely powerful, is surely undeniable. As we read of these and many other conversions the centuries seem to slip away and we are back in New Testament days. The methods by which the Message is, as it were, applied to the human heart differ with the individual, but this is thoroughly in accord with New Testament evidence and practice. Here in a few words a writer tells of radical changes in personality which cannot be explained away in purely human terms:

"God works in various ways. A young woman gave her testimony. She said that no one spoke to her; she heard God's voice in her own heart and was saved. Another woman told us that it was when she attended a meeting for fellowship that God convinced her and she was saved."

In translating the Letters of the New Testament I was frequently conscious of how St. Paul and the others took this change of human personality almost as a matter of course— they had seen it happen so frequently! It was certainly not merely that they had seen good-living people improved and given a true focus for their hitherto vague faith, although that certainly happened and, in the Acts especially, is part of the working out of the Good News. No, they saw not merely improvement and development, but complete conversion to Christ taking place even in the most corrupt and degenerate.

Those of us who have studied ancient history know that places like Corinth were notoriously evil, even by the debased standards of those dark days. Yet the power of Christ lifted and transformed men and women who were deeply sunk in the unspeakable filth of such places and turned them into shining saints. *This is happening today.* This is what I would particularly ask the critics of Christianity to explain. What effects this change? Can the non-Christian show the slightest evidence that he and his friends can so change human nature? Let them read these few important words from Africa:

"Some come to Christ from reasonably clean past lives; others have been lifted by the power of Christ from the deep mire of terrible sins. But in all alike who come to Christ there is a newness of life. We feel one with them and thank God for the refreshment and strength that comes to us from God through fellowship with such Christians."

Or these, also from Africa:

"Quietly, by ones and twos, some of our African friends are entering into the full experience of salvation and it is thrilling to see the beauty of Christ beginning to dawn in them."

Surely it is obvious to any unprejudiced mind that the "foolishness" of the preaching of the Cross is in our own day and generation effecting what modern man is powerless to do. It is changing evil men into good men. It is as simple and as profound as that.

Now clear and unequivocal as the evidence of the transforming power of the Christian Gospel undoubtedly is, it would be foolish, cowardly and dishonest to pretend that the whole Christian enterprise of establishing the world-wide Kingdom is simply the preaching of the Gospel on the one side and the conversion of human hearts on the other. A right relationship with God is indeed all-important, but it is only the starting point of cooperation with His Purpose for the wholeness of man. There are Christians in this and in probably every land who tend to concentrate upon their own spiritual experience, and their whole ambition is to see that such experience is shared by others. But this is altogether too cramped and narrow a way for the true follower of Christ to take. Because he is secure in his own salvation he has no justification for turning his back on the many problems which arise in our complex modern world. In the vastly accelerated progresses of our modern days it is nothing less than a tragedy if the Christian retires into his own pieties and refuses to give specifically Christian witness in the problems which bewilder modern man.

For myself I can be nothing but thankful that in many parts of the world a Church that might otherwise have become complacent and isolated is being "winkled out" and obliged to bring Christian insights to bear upon basic human problems. In a country such as our own which enjoys a government containing not a few Christians, the average Church member may feel that there is no need for him to do anything about problems of food, housing and medicine, for example. But there are many places in the world where the proper use of the land, the provision of water for irrigation, the active combating of disease, the struggle with centuries-old ignorance, the provision of even moderately decent housing and suchlike things, are matters of highest priority. It is a poor Christian who cannot see that God cares for the whole of man and who leaves the solving of these and a hundred other problems to the minds of those who do not know the Purpose of God. Thus, though the Cross is of course primarily the symbol

The Preaching of the Cross

of our reconciliation with God, it is also the mark of the cost
of faithful discipleship. We cannot avoid having the Cross
in our heads as well as in our hearts, and in the following
section we shall consider briefly a mere handful of the urgent
problems which confront the conscientious Christian who has
left the security of these shores and is standing where the
winds of change are blowing violently.

11

II

The Cross in Our Thinking

I HAVE been haunted for years by a saying of the late Oswald Chambers. He wrote in one of his devotional books, as far as I remember, "The Christian has no right to lurk in the bosom of Jesus because his thinking gives him a headache." These words seem to me to express most aptly a temptation which especially besets a certain type of Christian, and probably besets all of us from time to time. There are those whose religious experience is beyond question and whose heart-loyalty to Christ no one would deny, who are for ever making the attempt to oversimplify the problems of the growing Church. Such people are invariably well meaning, but their grasp of the complexities of certain human situations is defective. They cannot see that the answer to every question cannot be simply reduced to a matter of "surrendering it all to Jesus." Not only are the problems too deep and complex for any easy solution, but Jesus Himself, as the Gospels record, would not countenance any sentimental dodging of the issue. Frequently in the Gospels we read of men who approached Him with a query expecting an easy and simple answer, only to be given in reply a further heart- and mind-searching question. It would seem that Jesus insisted on men using the minds that the Father had given them. Many of us would prefer it to be otherwise; we would really prefer to dig deeper into the religious experience that we know rather than launch out into hard thinking and the risky working out of possible solutions. But we must not "lurk." The leading of the Spirit is forward and outward and never backward. The prayer and the thought, the conference and discussion, are all costly. There must be something of the Cross in our minds before we can say with any confidence, "It seemed good to the Holy Spirit and to us."

As the Church moves forward into new positions, as circumstances themselves change suddenly and even violently, problems which demand the highest practical wisdom appear and reappear. There is no easy way through and there is no simple solution. By consecrated minds, by humble seeking of the wisdom which cometh from above, as well as by sturdy God-given common sense, the Church must make its way forward. Consider some of these problems, which are contemporary, and it will be immediately obvious that there is no escaping the Cross in our thinking.

1. What is the Church's attitude to be in Moslem lands? Is there to be some attempt at *rapprochement* since there is much that is superficially common to Christianity and Islam? Or is the Church to insist that "there is none other Name given amongst men whereby we must be saved," and remain a small isolated and persecuted minority? It is impossible here to deal even sketchily with such a problem, but surely we can all see how, faced with the frightening advances of atheistic Communism, many Christians feel there may be a

way of joining forces with those who at least strongly believe in the one God and, what is more, allow their faith to guide and control their lives. Other equally conscientious Christians are convinced that there should be no suggestion of compromise over the Truth revealed in Jesus Christ, and manfully they stick to their guns.

Do we at home realize what sort of problem may easily arise for the Moslem who becomes a Christian? His conversion may be perfectly genuine, but so closely knit is the Moslem community and so deep is its devotion to the Moslem faith that he, the newly born Christian, will find himself completely cut off from his former relations and relationships. He will lose his wife and family, possibly even his life. Employment will prove almost impossible in the Moslem community, and practically the only way in which the convert can live at all is as a servant under the Mission's roof, or else he must go to some country where the community is not predominantly Moslem—and neither of these solutions can be considered satisfactory.

Sometimes in a Moslem community the Church has built up, largely through its hospital work, a considerable weight of popular goodwill toward Christianity; but even here to make a full and open acknowledgment of Jesus as Lord and Saviour is very rare, and many of those who are most friendly toward the Mission seem quite indifferent to the need for any such open witness. Some local Christians may blame the methods of the Church. If only it had provided "schools, and more schools, and still more schools," and "had been able to bind the young as it were to the Christian community," they would not have been left in the position of "a small vulnerable minority." When the missionaries point out that one cannot make real Christians that way, the reply is: "That is your way; it is not ours: the Mission has failed to understand us." Such problems as these certainly mean a Cross in our thinking and call for the highest consecration of mind as well as sensitivity to the leading of the Spirit.

2. Now let us consider a very different problem which naturally arises wherever the Gospel is proclaimed, but which seems to be especially conspicuous in West Africa. "They find honesty according to our standards so hard, not only to practice, but even to conceive," writes one missionary. "And, whatever they do, they want a tangible and sure reward, for they are born traders, in things material and spiritual. . . . After a discussion on bribery, which all the girls agreed was the curse of African public life, one of the prefects got up: 'It is no use pretending we shan't bribe. We must, to get anywhere. When I leave school I shall bribe myself right to the top, and then I'll show everyone how a Christian ought to live.' In one of the lower forms, after a study of the martyrdom of Stephen, one of our catechists' daughters put up her hand: 'But what I *still* don't understand is—what exactly did Stephen *get* out of being stoned?' "

Such naïve and revealing remarks as these may easily horrify us at home. But of course it is no use merely being horrified. We have got to envisage in our thoughts and prayers a situation where bribery is as much a part of the social system as "tipping" is in our own. In both cases the practice is deplored and yet accepted by most people. In Nigeria in particular vast numbers of people are responding vigorously to ever widening opportunities and are filled with a boundless ambition "to get on." We can easily see how difficult it is to teach self-giving service and devotion to any cause that does not yield immediate returns. That the witness of the Church must continue patiently and faithfully goes without saying, but we at home ought sometimes to visualize the difficulties of proclaiming a non-profit-making Faith such as Christianity among hundreds of thousands of people excited with opportunity and fired with heady ambition.

This problem may arise not merely in West Africa but wherever there is a sudden awakening to fresh opportunities and ways of life, as is shown by this extract from a letter written from another part of Africa altogether:

"It is against this background of easy money for those who are not too scrupulous, of a good deal of ostentatious display from among the more wealthy and of the fear of criticizing what is wrong in case it brings trouble, that we have to try to let in the light of the Gospel and teach the meaning of the Cross to young people who are naturally attracted by what is offered by the new conditions."

Unquestionably this whole problem of honesty and disinterestedness is basically a problem of the heart. But how to present and teach the values of Christian society calls for the strenuous use of human minds.

3. It is obvious that Africa is a quickly awakening continent, and equally obvious that nothing can hold back her material progress. Western ideas, Western amenities, and Western industrialization are all strongly influencing young, emergent Africa. At the same time thousands upon thousands of educated Africans are becoming increasingly aware of themselves and of the greatness of their country. Doubtless they are willing to borrow much from Western sources, but they are equally convinced that they have their own proper development to make along African lines. Again, one is pain-

fully conscious that this is far too big a problem to be dealt with in a small book such as this, but some of the problems must at least be indicated. For instance, to take Nigeria again as an up-and-coming country, responsibilities are being thrust into the hands of Nigerians with frightening rapidity. In effect, they want to be free, free to make their own mistakes in their own way. This may seem to us very adolescent, but it is surely part of natural development, especially as they are working toward self-government. But what is the missionary who loves Africa and the Africans to do in such a rapidly changing atmosphere? Will the old loyalty to the Church or Mission stand the strain of such revolutionary change of circumstance? Is it the missionary's duty to enter as far as he can into the sphere of local government and politics and so help to guide the inevitable forward march?

Then there is the problem of education in rapidly changing Africa. In most African territories today the demand for education is immense and unsatisfied; yet only a minority of African children in most areas has the chance of any education at all. Even so, some Christian educationists who know Africa well feel that for the Church the right policy is to concentrate on the fullest education of what, with limited resources, can only be a privileged few. At first sight this appears monstrously unfair and even un-Christian, but we must consider what is likely to happen if the Church pursues a policy of quantity rather than of quality. It means a very little education for a great many. It means starting a process of knowing and wanting to know more—arousing a hunger which in most places neither Church nor State has yet the means or manpower to satisfy. It means Africans moving into surroundings of Western industrialization with a minimum of education that often proves quite insufficient to enable them to adjust themselves to a life so different from their village tribal life. Would they not be better men and happier men, even if poorer men in the material sense, left as uneducated tillers of the soil? These again are problems to which there is no ready and easy answer, but since the Church is relatively so small it certainly looks as though it is a better thing to concentrate on quality rather than on quantity.

Then of course there is the problem of "education" itself. These words from Kenya are most illuminating:

"Education is advancing at a rate which can only be termed 'alarming.' . . . But the disquieting feature is the only too apparent endeavour on the part of the teacher and pupil alike to get and impart knowledge, not for what it is and what the person who has it can give, but what, as a so-called educated man, he can *get*, viz., wealth and status. . . . The well-educated African is dressing better and living better. But the paradox seems to be that the children are by and large no better cared for, except that every endeavour is made for them to get to school. Even among the well-to-do, matters of diet, adequate clothing, adequate housing, and necessary hygiene are still lacking."

And here are some more words, written this time from Uganda, which vividly illustrate the present situation:

"Here they are, these past pupils scattered over the country, these 280 girls now in schools: and what are they spreading over Uganda? A knowledge of homecraft and mothercraft, a knowledge of history, mathematics or biology? The spirit of self-giving service to their people? The capacity to see situations and judge clearly for themselves? But without the knowledge and acceptance of the Saviour for themselves

18

these things are of no value either to themselves or to their country—and there's the challenge to us. For it is in the reality and sincerity of our daily contacts with these girls, these women, and the spirit in which all work is done in the school, that Christ can be made known to them. It may be that we have to accept for ourselves the pain, the shame, the loneliness, the exhaustion that went with the Cross—to help those with whom we work to understand that the Cross means these things for the Christian—before the joy and power of the Resurrection can come with Christ's forgiveness to change the lives of these girls, and to change the country of Uganda."

Behind the obvious sincerity and concern of such words we can easily see the danger of mere "education" to coming generations of Africa. We have not to look very far here in the West before finding plenty of examples of people who are "educated" in the technical sense but who, spiritually speaking, have not even begun to be educated in the ways of the Kingdom of God. We in the West who call ourselves Christian nations, God forgive us, are in many ways very poor examples for a lusty young nation breaking out at last from the prison house of centuries of fear and ignorance. Plainly nothing can halt the vast and growing appetite for "education," but only the Church of Christ can give education that quality of self-giving service, that willingness to give rather than to get, and that desire to spread light and knowledge as God's gifts to be used in accordance with His Plan. Humanly speaking, the resources and power of the Church are very small. The problem is how best they can be used in the present urgent pressing forward toward knowledge of countless people.

At the same time the Church must be thinking of the

future. In the past, magnificent work has been done by poorly educated catechists and Bible women. Probably no praise is too high for their faithful and devoted work given in return for almost negligible earthly reward. Many of them are still continuing to be useful, and no one can gainsay their Christ-like gentleness and patience. But before very long there will be educated people in hundreds of thousands for whom well educated teachers of the Gospel will be essential. The supply and training of such men and women is yet another problem for the forward-looking Church.

4. Here is another kind of problem, small in itself per-haps, but chosen because it is representative of the kind of practical problem with which the Church has to cope in a hundred different ways. There is frequently no precedent or tradition to serve as a guide, and the Christian leader must rely for wisdom upon the living Spirit as well as upon his own common sense. If we use our imagination we can see that quite far-reaching principles may be involved in a particular local problem, as the following quotation indicates:

"Occasionally a member of the congregation will get drunk on the local beer. This is sad, and disciplinary action is usually taken. But it raises a matter which, I think, the Church will have, sooner or later, to take into serious con-sideration. Some churches or bodies here make teetotalism a *sine qua non* of Church membership. But many of us think that this is not the right solution to the problem which at rock bottom is a social one. (Admittedly the vitamins which are essential to life are found in the local beer . . . it is rather interesting the way people seem instinctively to find a vitamin-giving food or drink. I am told that the Indians find these vitamins in their curries; here people don't eat curries, they drink beer.) Drinking provides a social intercourse for the folks in a tribe. Ought the Church to consider the possibility of baptizing into Christ these social parties at which beer is drunk? The prayer meeting is not the counterpart of these social gatherings. That is something different—a religious gathering. Social life is an essential part of a man's life . . . ought attempts to be made to eradicate a social custom so deeply rooted? (I am asking questions only—I don't pretend to know the answers.)"

Of course, in a given situation there are many factors to be considered. The Gospel is a Gospel of liberty, but the individual Christian has his responsibility toward "the weaker brother." We remember St. Paul's brave words over such a harmless practice as eating meat: "This makes me determined that, if there is any possibility of meat injuring my brother, I will have none of it as long as I live, for fear I might do him harm" (*I Corinthians* 8.13). The right combination of Christian liberty and deep Christian charity has to be found and applied afresh in many different situations by the living Church of today. This without any doubt means a Cross in the thinking of every conscientious leader.

5. I have left until last the many problems which are the aftermath of the Mau Mau Emergency. At the moment of writing the phase of violence and terror would seem to be over, but the task of "screening" the very large number of suspects, and the much larger task of rehabilitating, re-educating, and resettling many thousands of people is being energetically tackled. Obviously these processes, which are mostly in official hands, bring particular problems both to European and to African Christians in Kenya.

It is not part of my present work to tell the most moving

story of almost unbelievable courage shown by Christians in Kenya under the threat of mutilation and death, but I feel I cannot pass on to the problems created by terrorism without at least paying tribute to all those magnificent Christians who, despite pressures and threats hardly credible to us here at home, refused to deny their Lord. Many of them paid for their faithfulness with their lives, and as I have read these reports of superhuman heroism I have yet again felt myself back in spirit with the Young Church in action.

But what of the problems left behind by the receding tide of violence? There are far too many to catalogue all of them, and I must rest content with setting down a few. These quotations will, I think, speak for themselves:

a. "In the earlier days of the Emergency, the Cross spelt persecution and death for the Christian. That phase is now over, but opposition, conflict, suffering, misunderstanding, remain with them. In a sense it is easier to face imminent danger than to be forbearing when the danger lessens, and their loyalty is not recognized, and a multiplicity of restrictive regulations frustrates them at every turn. . . . They are ridiculed and hated by those of their own tribesmen who are still embittered Mau Mau, and they are often distrusted by the Government whom they try to serve. . . . I am constantly humbled by their patience and lack of bitterness which springs clearly from an acceptance of the Cross in their lives."

b. "Nearly all the Kikuyu have now been moved into new villages. This is a measure which has general support, from a security point of view. . . . But there is a big price to pay. They used to live in private homesteads, and the more progres-

22

sive had made very attractive places, demonstrating their own individuality. When the fighting phase is nearly over suddenly to be ordered to pull down their homes and to rebuild, often in a universal pattern, cheek by jowl with those who do not share the same outlook . . . gives some idea of the cost. . . . What in fact is happening is the urbanization, to some extent of the whole tribe, and a completely new set of social relationships forced upon them."

In one district "the Christians asked to be allowed to build by themselves, and not be herded in with the majority who are Mau Mau sympathizers; an understandable desire, though not the outgoing attitude that being a 'redeeming society' demands. The District Commissioner told them that he wanted them to go in with the rest to act as leaven. Shortly afterwards, one of the villages was punished for feeding a gang, and a twenty-three-hour curfew was imposed, and the Christians were not allowed to go to church in the next village— for there was no church in their own. . . . It was irksome . . . to be punished just like the rest; it indicated that no more confidence was placed in them than in anyone else. . . . Things of this sort are constantly happening, and the Christian bears the Cross of the misbehaviour of his fellows."

c. "The Church's essential contribution is not always understood, but *we* know that unless we bring the Message and Challenge of the Cross faithfully our work will not be deep enough to meet the full needs. The Message of the Cross has a far wider implication than personal salvation of individuals; the mind has to be stretched to see the whole of life redeemed and that means moving out from the relatively calm waters of a limited personal devotion into an endless sea of service to the community. As yet few of our Church members realize that they are being summoned to launch out into the deep."

d. "The stumbling block of the Cross is clearly seen in all camps where redemptive work is based on the Christian Message. Detainees will confess a bit, and then a bit more—just as much as they think they must to obtain release. They will wriggle as much as possible to avoid coming fully into the open. Apart from the challenge of Christianity I do not know how one can be sure that the man has really determined to start a new life. But when a man accepts the implications of the Cross, then confession becomes complete and there is a solid basis for reconstruction."

e. "It is evident that these keen Christians not only preach by their lips and lives the salvation that they are continually experiencing at the foot of Christ's Cross, but also, though mostly loyal and innocent of any Mau Mau connexion, they have to bear daily their own cross of suffering and inconvenience. . . . Only this week our clergyman shared with me his concern for the 'saved' Christians in a nearby new village where in the last few weeks five of these people have been badly beaten without cause by an 'ex-Mau Mau,' now a Home Guard, who hates them because they are witnessing Christians."

In addition to these brief but vivid glimpses of the sort of crosses which our Kikuyu brethren in Christ are being called on to bear both mentally and physically, there are two other problems which the Church as a whole has to think out carefully. The first is the problem of receiving back into the fellowship of the Church those whose faith and courage were not equal to the Mau Mau terror and who, in consequence, explic-

24

itly or implicitly denied their Lord. This is no fresh problem for the universal Church, for this unhappy situation has arisen from time to time since the earliest days of Christian persecution. But that does not make it any easier or less painful for the Kikuyu Church to decide exactly on what terms they can receive back those Christians who failed in the hour of trial.

The second problem which arises is that in the wake of the Mau Mau terror there come all sorts of well meaning people willing to spend a great deal of time and money in re-educating, rehabilitating and rehousing Kikuyu people. It is almost bound to seem to many Kikuyu that the net result of all the trouble and terror is that they are receiving far more attention and, in some cases, far better conditions than if they had remained quietly loyal people!

A correspondent to the *East African Standard* wrote:

"Only this week I came across a family of three young Kikuyu children who were a pitiful sight. The youngest was too weak to walk; the others could walk but were desperately thin: they shivered as they clutched a few square inches of rag about their emaciated bodies. Their crime? Their father was a Christian teacher who had opposed Mau Mau from the beginning and paid for it by being murdered in 1953. A few minutes after leaving this family I passed a 'Works Camp' for Mau Mau detainees; the inmates looked well fed, and were smiling, as well they might."

We can easily see that it is no easy task for the Christian teacher to explain, in face of the evidence, that rebellion and disloyalty are in fact evil things.

Any thoughtful reader will see from this short chapter that the actual application of Christianity to human life bristles with problems. I repeat that in many cases there are no easy solutions, and much careful thought coupled with earnest prayer must be cheerfully given if Christian solutions are to be found. We must not attempt to avoid the Cross in our heads any more than in our hearts.

III

The Cross in the Pains of Adjustment

ONE OF the problems that are sometimes oversimplified by the not so thoughtful is the problem of learning to live together. In theory and on paper it is fatally easy to expound the brotherhood of man, but as soon as the theory begins to be put into practice all kinds of practical difficulties begin to emerge. Differences of background, habits of thought, manners and speech are more deeply ingrained in most of us than we realize. So long as we move among those with a similar background, with similar values, there is no problem worth mentioning. But the moment we move out of our familiar surroundings and have to live among people of a different cultural inheritance, people whose very thought and vocabulary are alien to us, we see at once how acute is the problem of living together. We certainly need not go overseas to find hundreds of examples of the difficulty of establishing fellowship with people whose mental make-up is differently constituted from our own. Any young curate who is moved from a suburban London parish to an industrial city in the north will well understand what I mean. Equally the northerner or the midlander will frequently find himself ill at ease and even desperately unhappy in, shall we say, one of England's south-western towns.

Every year thousands of our young men who are drafted into Her Majesty's Forces realize afresh the widely differing attitudes or habits of mind which coexist even in our own small island. We have got to be intensely realistic over this practical difficulty. It is only too easy to preach sermons and write articles about the "Brotherhood of Man" and be quite unable to live in fellowship with people next door or in the flat below. At this point there comes the temptation for Christians to say that the whole problem would be solved if only all men were Christians. Unhappily that is not true to experience. God has made people so different, not only in their capacities and gifts but in their temperamental attitude to life and in their vision of truth, that even those who sincerely love our Lord Jesus Christ have to make painful personal adjustments in order to work and live together in fellowship.

I want to refer back for a moment to the Young Church. We have probably all read many times in the book of the Acts, chapter 4, verse 32, the words: "The multitude of them that believed were of one heart and of one soul." This is the kind of phrase which, if we have not got our wits about us, can pass us by without our realizing its significance. We can so easily imagine the early tiny Church being a small band of people with similar experience who were quite naturally of one heart and soul. We need to remember that by this time the Young Church numbered several thousands, that it consisted of people from all parts of the Roman Empire who had been converted on the Day of Pentecost and later. There would by no means have been the same cultural heritage nor indeed would their actual habits of living have been identical. Moreover, it is doubtful whether it could be argued that even their spiritual experiences were all equal. There were those of course who had known Jesus Christ personally, who had to a man deserted Him at the time of His arrest, but who had later witnessed the unforgettable demonstration of the Resurrection. These would have been a minority; many would have been Jews and proselytes from the far corners of the Empire, who had only recently realized that God had in fact visited and redeemed His people in Person, and who had turned to Christ through the fearless and vigorous witness and obvious vitality of the Church. To me at least it is one of the major miracles of those early days that such a mixed collection of people could be soberly described by St. Luke as being of one heart and soul.

The explanation of this miracle is surely that their common experience of the living Christ was so rich and real that their very acute differences in other ways became insignificant. Now I cannot imagine for one moment that in that first fresh lively fellowship there was complete identity of spiritual experience. I can readily imagine the fresh Wind of Heaven blowing away pride and prejudice, but I cannot imagine the same free Spirit steam-rolling these early Christians into a flat robot-like uniformity! If the truth makes men free, if there is liberty where the Spirit of the Lord is, then those men were much more their true selves, in all the glorious variety of insight, temperament and ability that God had given them, than they had ever been before. Their unity lay at the deepest possible level—that in heart and mind they were utterly devoted to Christ and fully open to His life-giving Spirit. Such unity is a miracle, but it happened, does happen, and can happen again.

Now problems of working together in fellowship are continually arising, and the facile answers are false. It is no good, for example, denying the very real and radical differences that exist between people even when they are of the same race, and that is obviously a difficulty which is exacerbated very greatly when different races and cultures mix together. Neither is it any good for those who enjoy an intense but narrow religious experience to imagine that all problems of working together in fellowship would be solved if only all men had a spiritual experience identical with their own.

It does not need much imagination to believe what one has often been told—that the sharpest pains of personal adjustment await any foreigner as soon as he arrives at the place to which he has been sent to serve in a strange land. There are certain obvious physical and mental adjustments to be made, and for these he is probably prepared, but even the best training in the world can hardly prepare him for a situation where his whole previous concept of himself is not even considered. At the back of his mind, despite all his training, there may easily be lingering the thought that he, especially if he be a white man, is really being "jolly decent" to make the sacrifice of spending his life among his "backward" brethren! But he may soon find that he is regarded by some as an unwelcome intruder; he may be set to work in a junior position under a "colored" superior; he may even be shown up in his pride and prejudice and even suffer the ignominy of not being considered a true Christian at all! I do not think that we at home should ever forget in our thoughts and prayers this kind of adjustment which has to be made in greater or less degree by all who serve Christ in another country than their own.

Another adjustment that may need to be made is in one's attitude to the sin of denominational divisions. I sympathize very strongly with anyone who longs for the reunion of the Christian Church. When one considers all the highly organized powers of evil arrayed against the Church it seems little short of madness to perpetuate our divisions. That reunion will come is absolutely certain, but meanwhile those who long and pray for it have to bear a very real cross in adjusting themselves to meet in charity those who cannot see the clamant need. Here are two letters illustrating the strength of denominational feeling. The first comes from Asia:

"In January we were delighted to be joined by Miss X., who gave up the post of Sister-Tutor elsewhere to come and join us here. She even took over the Clinic and is running it well, and she has also taken responsibility for the Sunday School and Women's Meeting. . . . She is a very keen Christian and a great help in many ways. I was appalled at the Clergy Meeting after the last Synod that someone should have got up and objected to non-Anglicans working with us in the villages; and I said a good deal at the time! When the Anglican Church here can produce people like Miss X. it will be beginning to get somewhere."

Similarly, from Africa we read:

"In this area both Anglicans and Methodists are at work. The midwife is an Anglican and runs her clinic in the Anglican Church. To the people who attend I am sure denominationalism means nothing. . . . I put the case to our advisory committee for us to approach the Methodist Church and build a united Christian Maternity and Health Centre there, but all the African members turned it down and tried to persuade us to keep the clinic a specifically Anglican one."

It should be noted that the protest comes from the local Church itself. I also note particularly the sentence "to the people who attend I am sure denominationalism means nothing," and I could find hosts of parallels to that in my own experience in this country. Many people are hungry for God, many people long to know the transforming power of Christ, but outside the Churches themselves probably not one person in a million cares two straws about the niceties of the differences which divide Christ's Church. I wonder how long it will be before the Church itself realizes this, and further realizes honestly what an uprush of joy and spiritual power follows, despite all the pains of adjustment, when the Church is in fact united, as in South India.

A fine attempt to overcome prejudice and open wide the doors of Christian fellowship comes in another report from Africa:

"After our first few weeks here it was suggested to us by some of the members (Europeans) of the congregation that we should put up a notice-board outside the Church, 'European Church.' We were not surprised at this request and I made it quite clear at a general meeting of the congregation that 'All Saints' ' was to be the Church for 'all saints.' . . .

"Many of our African Christians however, living in All Saints' parish, are still very reluctant to meet with us for worship . . . chiefly because from the beginning it was regarded as the 'European Church.' Nevertheless, the number of Africans worshipping with us is slowly increasing and 'All

Saints' ' Church is beginning to be true to its name. Africans —ministers in government and senior service officials—English, Scots, Irish, Welsh, Swiss, South Africans, West Indians, Anglicans, Methodists, Presbyterians, Baptists, Salvationists, Congregationalists, Plymouth Brethren—all these nationalities and denominations are represented in our small church."

We can readily imagine that such a bold venture was not achieved without opposition, and that there are continual pains of adjustment in such Christ-like comprehensiveness.

Even those who are keenest on the reunion of Christ's Church will not pretend that it is an easy task. Through the centuries rifts of division have gone deep, and much patience, forbearance, good humor and the fullest understanding are necessary for our painful forward progress. From a united theological college we can catch a glimpse of some of the difficulties which call for these qualities:

"While the sense of fellowship in the Holy Ghost is very strong, there are inevitably some minor tensions. For instance, when a man is the only representative of his tribe there is always some sense of loneliness, not only because of difference of temperament but even more with having no one with whom to converse in his own language. . . . Some men seem to feel this more than others. . . . Then again it is very difficult for our non-Anglican friends, being small minorities yet having an almost equal stake in the college, not to be overassertive in order to preserve their identity."

Many of us will have read an article in the November 1955 issue of *Church Illustrated* called "Front Line in Malaya," written by the Bishop of Singapore. Here we have the Church illustrating in a small but highly significant way happy cooperation between different nations and different races and, what is sometimes quite as difficult, different missionary societies working happily together. The bishop writes:

"We are at work in five capitals. I have already mentioned Malaya's two capital cities, Singapore and Kuala Lumpur. But the diocese covers also English-speaking congregations in Indonesia, Thailand and Viet Nam. In two of their capitals we have churches and chaplains, Djakarta and Bangkok. In Saigon we worship in the French Protestant Church.

"These congregations are among the most cosmopolitan in the world. In them East and West join freely. At one Confirmation in Bangkok there were candidates from Canada, China, England, India, Thailand, Switzerland, Australia. It matters not only that far from home the British should find their own Church awaiting them, but that through its worship and life by men, women and children of many nations, witness should be given to Christ in a non-Christian country."

We can readily imagine the pains of adjustment involved here, but surely such united witness and worship is enough to make the very angels rejoice! I could wish with all my heart that all those churchy-minded people who hold back the inevitable realization of reunion would at least read of the actual situation in which the Church finds itself in non-Christian countries. Should not this paragraph from Central Travancore make any Christian's heart burn within him?

"Our relations with the Sister Churches in the area have been most cordial. We have an actual week of witness in September when we join hands with the Mar Thoma Church and the Salvation Army in evangelistic work among non-Christians. We long for the day when there will be a closer fellowship and greater participation in giving a united front to the non-Christians around in Christian worship, Christian witness and Christian work for the greater glory of God and effective presentation of the Lord Jesus Christ as Messiah, Mediator and Master."

Most of us are conservative by nature and do not take kindly to radical changes. But if the young Church is flexible and resilient it adapts itself to changed outward circumstances cheerfully and does not waste time in shedding tears over past glories. Nevertheless, there is bound to be a certain pain in the change-over, especially if it means an apparent decrease in importance. Let us read sympathetically these few words from India:

"One's first reaction to Sikandra is *Ichabod*—the glory is departed. The ruins of houses and other buildings and the general state of disrepair were most depressing. Also most people talk of Sikandra in the past—the once flourishing Press, the Industrial School with its carpentry, weaving and tailoring departments, the school and the orphanage, and one realized that Sikandra must cease to live in the past and adapt itself to new conditions. . . . Sikandra is a set-up belonging to the old spacious and moneyed days, but there are still parts of the work which can be used for its original purpose, the Press, the Hostel, the School. They are full of young lives which may be brought into touch with 'Jesus Christ and Him crucified.' The outward circumstances of a mission station may change, its financial state may deteriorate, but in each generation there is one condition that is always present, and that is lives to be won for Christ, a far more important thing than bricks and mortar."

These are words of brave common sense, but it is by no means easy to "decrease" even if the purpose is that the essential work of Christ may "increase."

Again, since we are all frail and faulty human beings, there are bound to be pains of adjustment in fitting in with one another. These next words seem to me to be full of sweet reasonableness. That we are basically "all one in Christ Jesus" is surely no excuse for ridiculing the reticences and assaulting the personality of a fellow Christian.

"Personal relationships—these are obviously vital. But I cannot help feeling that often not nearly enough attention is given at the start to the ordinary methods of common sense and good manners. Deeper relationships can and do follow, if real love is there, but to attempt to get to these levels by force is to commit a breach of good manners, put their backs up and lose ground. The application of the ordinary conventions allows people to get to know and like each other and to trust each other. This really does make a grand foundation for getting to the deeper levels without which a missionary team cannot work together."

In the sphere of personal relationships one of the very real crosses that has to be borne by some missionaries is the difficulty of adjusting to the "brethren" of the Revival Movement in Africa. I have met something like their counterpart here in this country. It is most emphatically not easy for some people to enjoy fellowship with those by whom the ordinary God-given reticences and normal conventions of polite society are almost certain to be interpreted as compromises, hypocrisies or sins. For myself I have no great liking for "spiritual nudism"; one has, however, to remind oneself constantly that these "brethren," narrow though the experience and outlook of many of them may seem to be, have a real and deep devotion to Jesus Christ. What is more, they have often succeeded in winning to Christ men and women where more conventional methods have signally failed. But let a missionary write of his difficulty in making the adjustment of Christian fellowship:

" 'An open mind' is hardly the sort of attitude the 'brethren' find easy to understand or honour. Holding back is too readily taken for fear, unwillingness to repent of some sin or sins, or (they put it like this quite openly) evidence of not being a Christian at all. . . .

"What are we to say to these things? Instinctively one objects to the narrow views often expressed among the 'brethren.' As both an Englishman and an Anglican one finds it none too easy to sit in a meeting for an hour singing over and over again, between testimonies, the same chorus in Luganda. Yet there remains the undoubted fact that most of the best Christians in the Church here are in the Fellowship. However hard we find it to bear with their ways of expressing themselves, these men have sought to take seriously the claims of Christ on their everyday lives in a way that is not always evident outside their number. . . . I cannot see how we can hope to help or influence these our brothers by outside criticism. They just cannot accept it, and we have to reckon with the fact and to act accordingly. It does not make it any easier to bear with what we see to be errors or short-sightedness within the Movement. But it does leave the door open for a contribution to be made towards rectifying these things, if we are humble enough to pocket our pride for now, and to walk humbly with these Christians who have much to teach us. . . . Just here for us the Cross comes right home."

I find the humility, the reasonableness and the willingness to learn which arises from these words most moving. And I think I can imagine the prayer at the foot of the Cross which alone enabled them to be written.

Other problems arise because the preaching of the Gospel inevitably carries with it the raising of the status of both men and women. Through Christ they are now sons and daughters of God, which, as St. John reminds us, is no mere courtesy title but a sober statement of fact. This new conception in turn inevitably leads to the question of the relationship between the sexes. We all know what is the ideal, and we all know what should happen, but rigorist attitudes are nearly always harmful, partly because they do not really solve problems and partly because rigorists themselves are so often astoundingly lacking in wisdom and charity. I earnestly beg all those who have a cut-and-dried answer to problems of sex morality to read what may be quite new to them—Christ's recorded words in *St. Matthew* 19. 10–11. Here now are some words from West Africa on the subject of polygamy, a problem which the Church has to face in many fields:

". . . the fact is that so many, even Christians, are polygamous. . . . I have tried to think a little about this and I wonder if we are not trying to go too fast? . . . In the first place we've been used to monogamy for hundreds of years now, the people here haven't. Why should we expect them to change overnight? Further, their polygamy does answer certain needs, as the desire of every woman is to marry and have children, and again [there is] the complete lack of any conception of spinsterhood and what to do with it. Shouldn't a move to heighten the concept of womanhood come first?"

The Cross in the Pains of Adjustment

Let us not be horrified at this fresh-eyed comment. We all know a one-man—one-woman lifelong relationship is the Christian ideal, but how do we apply it in practice to those to whom it is a new and even quite shocking idea? Do we say to the man who has nine wives and then becomes a Christian that he is to cast off eight of them to drift in a community which is not in any way prepared to receive them, since unmarried women are unknown? Here again some painful thinking has to be done, partly as to how the adjustment to the Christian ideal can best be made, and partly as to how we are "to heighten the concept of womanhood." Before we feel complacent and superior to the obvious disadvantages of polygamy, we might well reflect whether we in the West have made a conspicuous success of monogamy! A hostile critic could easily point to our huge divorce rate and the very large number of unmarried women who are unhappy and frustrated.

From busy, overcrowded Hong Kong comes, not unnaturally, a note of some of the tensions Christians must inevitably face:

"Under the Cross means living under tension. That, as applied to a school, implies that we are not just trying to give academic education to hundreds of students, but a real Christian education with all that that conveys. But let us be honest and realistic in recognizing that in the modern, hustling, bustling examination-conscious world, that is not the reason why our students choose to enter our school. Even so, once they have entered it, we have to present the challenge of living under the Cross to them. . . . Shall we ignore these [government] rules in living under the Cross? Shall we ride rough-shod through them all as we go forward to interpret the Message of the Crucifixion? But we must remember that the Cross was planted firmly in history. We cannot escape the tensions created by the city in which we live."

The cheering thing about this brief extract to my mind is the honest facing of the situation as it is. The Cross was indeed "planted firmly in history," and in Christ's own life there were limitations, and no doubt regulations, which He made no attempt to evade. He accepted the "givenness" of the particular situation in which the Father had set Him. The servant is not greater than his Lord; we no more live in an ideal world than He did. What we have to decide, as He did, is how to do the Father's Will in the given situation whatever the cost to heart or mind.

Obviously there are scores of problems which confront the advancing Church, and the headaches cannot be avoided. Probably within measurable time—possibly even within a few years—European leadership, which is already diminishing, may have to disappear entirely. From Singapore we take a few significant sentences from a report:

"It seems to us very doubtful how long Europeans who look to England, Australia, or America as their homeland can remain in positions of authority in Church or educational institutions. Many of us realize this, and would be happy to see Asians in positions of authority but there aren't yet enough people suitable for these positions. . . . All this points to what I feel should be the number one priority in all our work, the training of local people for church work."

The particular pain here lies not only in the searching for leaders and the proper training of them, but in the disturbing fact that many people are quite blind to the signs of the times. Many of the reports I have read from various parts of the world show how tragically the Christian community can disintegrate and even disappear where there is no leadership, no shepherding of the flock. Since nothing can stop the march of events it would seem to me that the closing remark to this extract is profoundly true. There must be the "adjustment" of realizing what is happening or what is bound to happen, and "the number one priority" must be the training of leaders for the future.

IV

The Dodging of the Cross

PART OF the cumulative infection of this planet on which we live, part of what the theologians call original sin, is a tendency in all of us to avoid the difficult and unpleasant and take the line of least resistance if we possibly can. Of course, there are splendid exceptions to this tendency all over the world. But there are unquestionably millions of people who ingeniously evade mental or spiritual conflicts whenever they can, who almost instinctively avoid hard work either physical or mental and who take great care not to become involved in situations where they might possibly fail, or, worst of all, expose themselves to ridicule. I suppose we need not be surprised at such a widespread attitude in a sin-infected world, but it is particularly tragic and deplorable when it appears among professing Christians, when there is a wholesale dodging of the cost and pain of the Christian way of life. We can see such an attitude on all hands as clearly as we can detect at any rate a tendency to such an attitude in ourselves. But can we wonder at the ineffectiveness of the Church, at its timidities and cautious amateurishness, while so many of its members are knowingly or unknowingly avoiding the Way of the Cross?

The shining pristine vigor, the gay, unconquerable courage of the Young Church were not extinguished by hardship or persecution. Bitter opposition and fierce oppression in the first three centuries of the Church's life produced magnificent saints and a host of ordinary men and women to whom pain and persecution were accepted as part of the normal occupational risk of being a Christian. It was not opposition, it was not poverty or pain that sapped the fine athletic strength of the first Christian generations. It was the lack of opposition, it was prosperity and ease which led to a spiritual deterioration that all the violent persecution in the world could never accomplish. Fifteen hundred years ago the Roman Emperor Constantine became a Christian, and from then on it became perfectly safe and indeed highly fashionable to be baptized in the Name of Christ. Many regard that imperial conversion as a tragedy in the life of the Early Church, for, although it need not have been so, what actually happened as far as we can discover is that the bearing of the Cross largely disappeared from the lives of those who were baptized in the Name of the Crucified. "Nominal Christians" began to appear in vast numbers for the first time. It was altogether too easy to be "a Christian," and what the Church gained in numbers it more than lost in spiritual power and cutting edge.

Before long we find the Church rich and powerful, but almost entirely forgetful of its divine commission and of the divine way of redeeming the world. By the time of the Crusades, for example, it was considered a fine, manly Christian thing to go out and kill Turks in Palestine and drive them out from the Christian holy places. But who ever considered that the Turks were men for whom Christ had died and that the Church's job was not to kill them but to win them to God by the patient ways of the Cross? It was not for hundreds of years, except for a few isolated heroic endeavors, that the Church recovered, through its missionary societies, its true calling—to proclaim Christ and to bear His Cross before the whole world.

"Nominal Christianity," "Christianity without tears," may seem to have a certain limited virtue. Nominal Christians are frequently honest, kind and unselfish. To be fair, it is by no means always their fault that they are nominal Christians. Most of them have never been shown or taught that Christianity is inescapably the Way of the Cross, and that no person or situation is ever changed or redeemed without cost to someone. But, whether the nominal Christian is aware of it or not, he is in fact dodging the Cross, and in so doing becomes a stumbling-block to the newly converted and a brake upon the progress of the true Church of committed Christians.

The causes of nominal Christianity cannot always be explained by a conscious or unconscious "dodging of the Cross." Many people overseas were baptized as Christians with as little thought or knowledge of what really being a Christian might entail as the average English child who is brought to the front of his parish church. These words extracted from Bishop Leslie Brown's recent broadcast on "The Uganda Church" are most illuminating:

"In Uganda becoming a Christian meant taking over not other religious beliefs but the entire set-up of Western life. The new way brought by the Church—education, medicine, a money economy even, for we introduced cotton—meant material progress and a higher standard of living. You got your Christian name and showed you belonged to the new order through baptism, and so to baptism classes you went and became a Christian. We English people can't say much about that, for England was converted in much the same way, but if religion is only part of a set of conventions sooner or later it is going to be challenged and perhaps abandoned. People's desire for material prosperity hasn't abated in Buganda, but it is now realized that religion and the Christian life aren't essential to progress and may even be a hindrance sometimes."

It is very easy to see how in the past baptism frequently meant little more than linking yourself up with a way of living. I have no doubt at all that little if any blame can be attached to the missionaries who did the baptizing. But it is hard to see how the African could avoid concluding that, on the whole, becoming a Christian was "a good thing."

There will always be a danger of nominal Christianity where it obviously "pays" to be a Christian. But from Bishop Brown's words it is apparent that the situation is rapidly changing. Material prosperity need not now be received solely through Christian channels. Once again, as is always happening in the life of any Church in any land, the pattern of the Cross emerges. The bishop hints that it "may even be a hindrance sometimes" to lead the Christian life, and in this hint we can foresee that the period of nominal Christianity is passing and quite probably an era of real Christianity, carrying its own particular Cross, will soon appear.

Most of us would admit that unless we "take up our cross daily" our Christian witness slowly but surely deteriorates. Whatever the particular cross may be, if it be evaded by the members of a local church, the power of that church very quickly withers away. Here is a sad extract from a letter from a predominantly Moslem area in West Africa:

"But a more tragic reason for Christianity's failure lies in the lives of the Christians as seen by the upcountry people. Europeans and Africans alike are willing to admit that the drinking seen in lives of professing Christians, the compromise with Islamic and pagan customs, the personal dealings in business, etc. between Christians and non-Christians, does very little to commend the Gospel of our Saviour Christ to unbelievers. Our lives are watched very critically. . . ."

Here it is plain that the obvious cross which is being dodged is the pain of maintaining Christian standards. We at home should be slow to judge since we do not know at first hand the difficulties of living in predominantly Moslem or pagan surroundings. But, though we may be very conscious that we might not do any better ourselves, it is clear from the Christian observer on the spot that such evasion of the Cross "does very little to commend the Gospel."

In the same part of West Africa some nominally Christian teachers have discovered the fact that nowadays it is the Government that pays their salaries and not the Church. They are therefore under no obligation to the latter and if they wish to evade the Way of the Cross there is nothing to stop them. Here is a relevant extract from a letter from the same part of Africa:

". . . Some of our teachers were showing very little interest now in church work. I saw that only one of them was in church that morning. He [the pastor] says they come under the influence of teachers from other colleges who say: 'Why do you bother with all this church business? You are not paid for it. We are all government teachers now.' It is of course true . . . so that many of the teachers no longer think of themselves as servants of the Church or Mission and, unless they are truly servants of Christ, feel no obligation to do Christian service."

Of course, it is sad that some are throwing off their church loyalties so easily, but at least such a situation as this is showing up those who are really Christ's men as distinct from those who merely bore the label of Christian.

From another part of Africa comes a sad report; here the observer sees above all the failure to love. True love invariably finds a cross somewhere in its journey, and as we read these few words we can only conclude that somewhere along the road this particular mission station has wittingly or unwittingly evaded the cost of love.

"The first subject to occupy my thoughts is the witness of the Europeans in the station and I know that we stand condemned. The witness is dead, or the life in it is dim, and there is very little blessing. On our own doorstep we are not a saving community—and our love is not a strengthening and building one to each other. I often think the Africans must be bewildered by the gap between our profession and our life."

In another instance of church failure, this time from India, we can see how a Christianity that avoids the Cross can be a stumbling-block to others:

"It has been said more than once to evangelists during the course of personal work: 'We would become Christians but for the caste prejudices of the Christians in this village which would make it impossible for us to worship with them.' "

It is easy for us to see how thoroughly un-Christian is the caste system in India, and we may be eager to blame any Church which does not break with it. But it is not so very long ago that in our own country class distinctions were just as rigid, though not as elaborate, as caste differences in India. Very little voice was raised in the Church of England to point out the evils of snobbery, social pride and the idea that God Himself had arranged that people should be born in distinct social strata!

> *The rich man in his castle,*
> *The poor man at his gate,*
> *God made them, high or lowly,*
> *And ordered their estate.*

For how long has this verse been sung in our churches? Of course, two wrongs do not make a right, but at least let us look back on our own past history so that we may pray humbly and intelligently for a Church which has not yet fully broken with the rigidity of a centuries-old social tradition. Of course, it must have that courage, and the necessary humility. It will only discover the power of the Cross today by learning afresh the significance of the actual historic Cross.

From West Africa comes a different problem: "Here we have very few rationalists, atheists or agnostics—most men acknowledge God. . . . Because these people were taught in mission schools or because their parents were church members, they claim to be Christians. They are not Moslem, not heathen or pagan, and they have been 'taught' the Christian religion, hence nominal Christianity. The tragedy is that this church-going religion, masquerading as Christianity, bears little relation to one's job or even how one conducts one's life—hence the low moral standard of so many church members."

48

The Dodging of the Cross

Here is nominal Christianity in the mass, so to speak. How long it will last as a churchgoing phenomenon no one can say, but there seems to me hope in the fact that the same writer says "the churches are well attended." At least there is the opportunity to proclaim vigorously the difference between nominal Christianity and the real thing. Surely our prayers are urgently needed both for those who minister to these thousands of nominal Christians and for the minority of genuine Christians who live among them.

In our own country, despite much traditional Christian "hangover," we have only a small minority who attend church. One of the most important features of the recent Billy Graham campaigns was Dr. Graham's insistence that new converts should link themselves up with the fellowship of the local church. For although there are through force of circumstances many "lone Christians" in the world, it would appear to be God's normal plan to work in and through the fellowship of His Church. To abstain from Church fellowship in the ordinary way weakens both the Church and the abstaining member. We are only too familiar with such abstentions in this country, and our fellowcountrymen abroad, as might be expected, often take their abstention with them. What a tragedy it is that they do not realize what damage they are doing to the Christian cause! From many letters it is obvious that even today to many Africans the terms "European" and "Christian" are synonymous. What is the African going to make of a "Western Christian" who refuses to join the Church's fellowship, even on a most sacred occasion? I quote briefly from a letter from West Africa:

"We try to go up to the Government reservation once a week for a game of tennis; this gives us a break, and gives us contact with the other Europeans. They are all most friendly and hospitable but never come near the church. At Christmas I sent out a letter to everyone explaining the work we were trying to do and hoping they would feel they could join with us in our worship—and giving the times of the services. I put it all as agreeably as I could, but the result was nil."

"The result was nil," says our correspondent. In another sense he is undoubtedly wrong, for the result of such laziness, snobbery, or sheer indifference could never be nil. Indeed it is difficult to estimate just how much damage is done not only to the Christian Church but to Afro-European relations generally by such crass insular stupidity. But not all our "government exports" are of such poor and insensitive spiritual material. Another letter shows a more heartening insight into the situation of the Europeans' responsibility as Nigeria strides forward to self-government:

". . . a [European] friend of mine (in government service) said this: 'I am deeply concerned at our failure to give the African government officials living in our midst anything except good reports on files and invitations to cocktail parties, at a time when the fate of the country is in their hands; we, the Christian community, should be offering them a quality of Christian friendship and fellowship which will enable their deepest needs to be answered.' "

I call these words heartening because they are typical of a small but significant European minority who are alive to the rapidly changing situation, and who see that the West has far more to give awakening Africa than mere education or technology. It must be easy to evade responsibility for this giving, especially if one has no Christian convictions and is secretly a little piqued that the days of one's own importance are numbered. It takes a generous heart, and that usually means a Christian heart, to feel and express a real concern for an adolescent people bent on fulfilling their own destiny.

It is appropriate to insert here two very short extracts from Dr. J. C. Carrothers' lucid and fascinating report on *The Psychology of Mau Mau:*

"But one can say this: That if the general white population of this Colony cannot practise Christian principles in their dealings with their fellow-men, both white and black, the missionaries might just as well pack up their bags and go."

"Let us face the fact, therefore, that we have got something valuable to give, though we have not always realized what that something was. Let us also face the fact that this gift cannot be given by the missionaries unless we others aid them by living Christian lives."

It is a grievous fact, but an undeniable fact, that the plague of nominal Christianity seems to arise wherever it is safe to be a Christian. As soon as there appears a cost or risk in becoming a follower of Christ those who are Christians in name only are quickly shown up for what they really are. A missionary writes from the Upper Nile Diocese:

"There are some who come to the edge as it were, and then draw back. No, they say, we cannot pay the price. Let us just be good church members, law-abiding citizens, then nobody will be offended. But there is no cross in their message, no living Saviour in their testimony. . . . Africa is full of such Christians; we wonder sometimes just what kind of a gospel we have been preaching—perhaps a cheap variety that costs nobody anything."

We need to note the comment—"We wonder sometimes

51

just what kind of a gospel we have been preaching," and indeed that is the sort of self-reproach that any of us who preach or teach or minister would feel if our people began to fade away the moment the hint of a cross appeared. But it is not necessarily a matter for reproach, even though we must be careful in proclaiming the Gospel never to forget its implicit cost. I venture to think that the heart of Christ Himself must have sunk as He saw hundreds of people deserting Him as soon as He began to talk of "hard things." At the end, as He faced the Cross itself He faced it alone. He knew what was in man, and although they were incredulous, He could tell His nearest and dearest friends that they would all desert Him in the hour of His need. We do not read in the New Testament of superhuman courage until we come to the Spirit-filled life of the Young Church. Here the picture is changed indeed and we find men, whose personalities are open to the Spirit of God, witnessing fearlessly and cheerfully suffering ignominy, loss and persecution. Probably the only answer to the pernicious problem of nominal Christianity lies in a fresh outpouring of the Holy Spirit. For Christianity of the cheerfully self-giving kind is not a work of nature; it is a work of the Spirit Himself.

Most sensitive Christians are very anxious not to add to the number of nominal Christians, since they can do no good and may do infinite harm. Here are a few lines from a Hong Kong letter:

"It is easy enough in Hong Kong to drift into baptism. . . . I wondered, in the case of two or three who have since gone overseas to study, did they think that they would be more accepted if they went as Christians."

The writer goes on to say that the fears may indeed be groundless, for these particular young people had seemed "very convinced" about the reality of their faith. But the fear is there, as it is for all of us who are responsible for launching young Christians upon the world—lest we add to that monstrous army of embarrassment, the nominal Christians.

In India it may be that it will grow even more difficult to become and remain a Christian, and that those who take on so lightly the name of Christian will be obliged either to deepen their faith or to abandon it altogether. At the moment the pattern of Cross-evading Christianity appears in India with the same miserable marks as it does in other countries. Here, for instance, are a few words from Bhagalpur:

"And for the average Christian, whether man or woman, I do not think it is an exaggeration to say that their religion bears very little relation to everyday life. So many are just nominal Christians: selling their rice in a Sunday market or playing in a football match or entertaining relations, are so much more important than worshipping God. Religion seems to be a matter for church on Sundays—quarrelling, disunity, selfishness, pride, continue. . . ."

This unhappy divorce of faith from conduct is the unmistakable mark of Cross-evasion, of bogus Christianity.

It is not pleasant to write this chapter, to have to say in all honesty that the same vague, ineffectual Christianity which melts away at the first breath of Cross-bearing is as much a blight upon the Young Churches of the world as it is upon our Church at home. But facts must be faced, and we can neither think nor pray intelligently if we see life through the rosy spectacles of optimism. Opposition and persecution will quickly reveal the counterfeit nature of nominal Christianity but they will not change it. What is needed and what we should pray for, both for ourselves and for others, is a fresh "intake" of the love and joy and power of God.

V

The Cross as the Way of Reconciliation

ONCE WE accept the startling truth that this is a Visited Planet,. that the Man Jesus was in fact the Character and Person of God expressed in human terms, we have taken what is probably the biggest single step possible toward the understanding of the whole complex situation in which we find ourselves and which we call "life." It was because the Young Church had accepted this as it were vertical action of God crossing at right angles the horizontal line of human history that the story of the Acts of the Apostles rings with joyful certainty and an unquenchable *joie de vivre* of the spirit. Now men knew what God was like, now men knew the basic plan of God for humanity, now men were able to explore the boundless resources of God's living Spirit. They could never forget the resounding triumph of the Resurrection coming as it did hard on the heels of what must have seemed to the early disciples the utter eclipse of their hopes. Small wonder that these men went out preaching everywhere Jesus and the Resurrection!

Nevertheless, they knew well enough that at the very heart of their new and joyful certainty about God there lay the costly ignominy of the Cross. Their own redemption, the potential redemption of all mankind, had been accomplished by Christ's unique Act. Now for the first time in human history could a full and free forgiveness of the past and a reliable resource for the future be simultaneously proclaimed. Once they, or we, or any Christians in any age have accepted as fact that our God has been focused for us in Jesus, there could scarcely be a more penetrating and significant statement of the whole new position than the words of St. Paul when he wrote: "God was in Christ reconciling the world unto Himself, not imputing their trespasses unto them." The frightful deadlock caused by conscience in the enlightened Gentile and knowledge of the Law in the instructed Jew had been broken by God's own initiative. God had personally come to the rescue and reconciled man to Himself at awe-inspiring cost.

All this the Young Church knew, and their Gospel was a Gospel of reconciliation, but so closely were they attuned to the very movement of God's own Spirit that it is only on apparently rare occasions that we find them mentioning the fact that they themselves are heart and soul involved in what might be called the secondary work of reconciliation. The primary work had been done, the unique sacrifice had been made, by none other than the Son of God Himself. But what we might call the secondary work involved all the newly born sons and daughters of the Kingdom. No man can bear what Christ bore, but all who follow the Way of the Cross are born again to the cost and pain of reconciliation. The early Christians found, and joyfully and even gratefully accepted the fact, that they were inextricably involved in the work of reconciliation. The Church, now the Body of Christ, could not meet sin, ignorance, fear, misrepresentation or persecution without paying for it. In a very real sense God used them to reconcile the world unto Himself.

Now the basic facts of the human situation have not changed in the slightest. The way of reconciliation to which all true Christians are committed is inevitably a way of conflict, of stress and strain. But frequently the living out of that way may not be immediately obvious. We may have to use our imaginative sympathy as we read some of the following extracts, for the Cross-bearing is not underlined.

The situation in India calls not so much for a new technique as for a more searching and costly Christian living. In a letter from that country we read:

"We believe that to be vulnerable is a great and precious thing when we long to share with others our Lord and what He has done for us and for them. In India one can still, by buying land, building houses, and by the maintenance of a sufficiently big bank balance, make oneself superficially secure from those unknown forces which are always present in work which above all is concerned with personal meeting, with personal relationships. We love security as much as anyone but hope to have the guts to pray to be kept vulnerable.

". . . It is the claim of Christians that the Gospel comes with the power to make men one in Christ Jesus in that utterly new quality of fellowship which needed the new Greek word 'koinonia' to describe it. There you have the specific for a divided society. We *must* discover this fellow-

57

ship of 'belonging in Christ' in practical, down-to-earth terms of group living, working, and worshipping, if friends in this country are to say—'This is the thing. These people are not just talking about freedom, friendship, love, they are caught up in the thing.' . . . That power of koinonia of which we spoke earlier is a too unknown power of the Church and yet it is absolutely essential to our neighbours possibly being gripped by the Good News of Christ."

Alongside this truly adult piece of Christian living we may consider this picture of some women at a diocesan training college in Nigeria who are taking their first step toward real Christian koinonia:

"So I decided that a general house meeting was needed, where everything could be brought out into the open. Details of what was brought up are unnecessary here, but the comments of so many showed that God is at work, changing attitudes and hearts by the power of the Cross of Christ. After some argument about food (we stick firmly to communal feeding on principle) one woman suggested that I give them all their own money, and they'd feed themselves. The outcry against that being the answer was summed up by one of them, 'No, that's only pulling further apart, it isn't the answer for Christian leaders like ourselves.' And again, when after two hours I remarked that we were spending the whole morning on it and was there anything else that needed to come up, several of them said: 'This is more important just now than the time-table. We all know that quarrels and palavers spoil the work of all our districts, and we have come here to learn how, as future leaders of the women, to live together as Christians, and to get difficulties right because we all say we believe in the same Saviour.' "

For myself I read these words with great joy. For here is no picture of people adopting the white man's religion for what they can get out of it, and certainly no impression of people accepting with the head only the tenets of the Christian Faith. Christianity obviously means learning to live together, and that can happen only as individuals are changed by the power of the Cross and as the fellowship realizes the need for establishing and maintaining happy relationships with one another. Reconciliation of the soul with God, reconciliation of individuals within the Christian fellowship—these are the essential preliminaries before God can use the fellowship to reconcile the world to Himself.

Most frequently men and women discover true fellowship in tackling a job together, and sometimes the more difficult the job, the deeper the fellowship. All Christians loathe war, but many of us cannot help but remember gratefully the deep fellowship which arose in time of war and which we all enjoyed as we faced common hardship and danger. It seems to me that if Christians realized the everlasting nature of the spiritual war in which they are inevitably engaged their differences would seem less important and their fellowship would almost automatically become deeper. Already, of course, this does happen—in Christian medical work, for instance, where the common enemies are suffering, disease and death. Here are a few cheerful words, typical of many reports, from a hospital in Uganda:

"In the middle of all this stands Mengo Hospital, a bit old-fashioned, poor and shabby, but with a stability that comes from having outlived the storms and trials which have beset us over a period of years.

"During the upheaval of the last year or so in Buganda we

59

have been able by the grace of God to continue as usual nursing Africans, Europeans and Indians in the same hospital compound . . . in the dispensary we have Baganda working with others from the Lango tribe, from Toro, Teso country, and Ruanda, along with us Europeans, and we are a happy team."

On a smaller scale, perhaps, but of no less significance is this passage from a report of the adventure of living together in a boys' camp in Nigeria:

"The adventure of joint service, in clearing a leper woman's farm, adventure in joint discovery at an airport and in the river, adventure in sharing questions at lunch-time, and discovering truth by questions rather than by authority, all these introduced some of the dimensions of the life of a man in Christ. I am convinced that they and we learned what it means to be 'a man in Christ' quite as much by these means, as through worship and through daily tasks, choruses, quiet times, and the reading of the lives of Pioneers of the Christian faith. . . . If such relationships and also such follow-ups are vital in Britain they are doubly so in Nigeria under the hand of God."

It is this sense of adventuring together, shown here on a small scale, which surely needs to be recaptured by Christians all over the world. For we are in fact called to share together a great, joyful, hazardous and at times costly adventure—the immeasurable task of world-wide reconciliation. But there will be no recapturing of the sense of adventure and no effectual work of reconciliation unless Christians are reconciled one with another. For myself I should not be in the least surprised to learn that in the eyes of heaven the biggest single handicap to God's use of His Church throughout the world today is the lamentable lack of reconciliation between fellow Christians. But where the reconciliation has begun to take place, as in the Church of South India, there is a release of power and joy and an increased willingness to act as God's reconciling agents. Here are some words from that united Church:

"Above all, Christians, if they are to take part in Christ's reconciling work, must be reconciled to each other. And in the reunion of the Church there is not only the healing of the larger and more ancient divisions, but a challenge to a truer fellowship at the local level. There is a former Anglican group of congregations in a large South Indian city which has for two generations been a little island of Anglicanism in a predominantly non-Anglican area. The wish of this group to maintain its integrity and independence was as much due to social as to ecclesiastical factors, and there had to be a progressive dying to self before those congregations could be effectively incorporated into the United Church. . . . That now they are more fully committed to the larger fellowship is shown by their participation in the campaign to declare the Gospel to their whole city with visits to every house and street."

Plainly there has been an influx of divine love and wisdom here, and barriers have melted like ice before the sun. Let us quote again from South India:

"The fellowship and unity of the members of the diocese who have come from twelve different social levels is marvellous and only through the grace of the Holy Spirit has this been made possible. . . . The occasion of these celebrations [the centenary of the first baptism from the underprivileged] gave a wonderful demonstration of the transforming power of the glorious Gospel of Jesus Christ. Still there are many problems to be tackled. Only in the power of the Spirit can they find a right solution."

Can any sane Christian refuse to believe that here we have at work the reconciling Spirit of God? The gentle pressure of the same Spirit is of course at work everywhere, but frequently churchmen are far too much concerned to defend their particular *status quo* to notice it. Thank God, however, from time to time the pressure is felt and a further step toward unity is made. Here are heartening words from Egypt:

"The Fellowship of Unity came to life again last winter. . . . A meeting was arranged in our own cathedral hall, at which the two Coptic Orthodox representatives to Evanston reported on the meeting of the World Council of Churches there. One of them made the statement that 'the Coptic Church left the ecumenical movement at the Council of Chalcedon in A.D. 451 and rejoined it at Evanston in A.D. 1954.' There is so much fellowship among Christians of different communions that one wishes that there were more time to direct it into more constructive channels."

It is sincerely to be hoped that in all the acceleration of modern history it will not take a further 1,503 years before Christians, realizing the might of the armies arrayed against them, have the good sense to close their ranks and be reconciled one with another!

Here, in a few lines from West Africa, is a glimpse of the ministry of reconciliation at a personal level:

". . . It happens that I have to work very close to what is known as the lorry 'boy.' Vocationally I am not sent out to help lorry boys or masons, but students. Yet it is to the lorry boy and mason that Christ has been coming with a new

62

meaning, as a result of personal contacts, rather than to the students. . . . Looking back I am conscious of having been very happy here; so happy that at times I wonder if it is not selfish to enjoy such happiness!"

But of course there are many in the world-wide Church, as there are many in the Church at home, who are not ready to be personal reconcilers. It is to many people, alas, a much more attractive prospect to keep themselves unspotted from the world by remaining safely in the fellowship of the ninety and nine. The tendency to do this is in us all but it must be steadfastly resisted, and we must be willing to lose our lives (which includes our reputations) if we are to save them. No effective reconciliation takes place if the Church remains a mere rallying ground for the righteous.

We are familiar with this attitude among the righteous here at home, and it could probably be paralleled in most places where the Church has been established for any length of time. It is an old, old temptation, and even in the Young Church we remember how St. Peter, despite his experience of conversion and Pentecost itself, chose to play safe rather than take the risks of reconciliation. (See *Galatians* 2. 11 ff.) But surely today in the fast-changing, fast-moving and fast-developing world scene Christians are called far more to be active adventurous reconcilers than to be the static faithful.

Here from the troubled scene in Malaya are a few brief words—enough to show the urgent need for personal reconcilers. The force of the law may, and should, restrain evil, but it cannot change people. Only Christ can do that, and for His work He needs ambassadors of reconciliation:

"Subversive activities are at work in our midst but nothing is being done about it. The only way is to put good there to

63

display the evil and win the people's loyalty to something or someone higher. Who can do this but the ambassadors of Christ? All the Government do is to arrest a man when he has gone too far; they have no means or personnel to put in and teach them."

There is another side to reconciliation by the power of the Cross. Jesus Himself said, "Blessed are the peacemakers," and sometimes Christians are called upon not to stick up for their rights but to bear patiently and cheerfully what is unjust and hard to bear. Such action, simply because it is so unusual in a greedy competitive world, may be in itself an act of reconciliation. Here, briefly, is the story of a fine Christian from Kenya:

"A progressive contractor living just outside Nairobi, known to the Administration as loyal, was attacked last year, and there is a fine story of his wife's and his fearless testimony: 'We are not afraid of death in this house.' He was told to pull down his house and build in a nearby village; he asked about his store for building materials and was told that it could stay where it was. He moved to the village; and then the head man, who has no sympathy for Christians, sent men to break down his store, and his materials were left exposed to the elements and to looting. He sought redress, and got none. The answer? Christian forbearance and forgiveness. He accepted the challenge, and goes on his way rejoicing, instead of allowing the seed of bitterness to rob him of God's peace in his heart."

We do not know the end of that story yet, but because one man refused to become bitter and resentful, thereby bearing a cross in his own heart, it would not be in the least surprising to find in the months to come that his witness has

proved yet again that such an attitude is a tool of reconciliation.

But not all Kenya Christians, or Christians of any country
for that matter, are of such stature and quality. Here again
are some candid words on the situation as it is:

"The extreme sensitivity of the highly-educated African is
due mainly to his pride; he cannot be told that he is wrong
. . . it is well for us to note that the Kikuyu idiom for a proud
man is a 'black European.'

"Perhaps one result of the present Emergency has been
to show Africans that not all Europeans are even nominally
Christian. The issue is more clearly defined as being one of
personal response to Christ and His Cross. Only the European
who is humble enough to accept the shame of this nominal
Christianity can find real brotherhood with those he has
come to serve."

These words show clearly the need for real Christian reconciliation, which can be undertaken only by those whose own
hearts have been touched by the Cross. Nominal Christianity,
conventional European Christianity, and any other substitute
for the real thing are worse than useless. The situation here as
in all the world calls for men and women who are truly humble and truly loving and who have left their own reputations
at the foot of the Cross.

VI

The Cross as a Way of Life

THERE ARE, it seems to me, a fortunate few who accept the need for self-sacrifice with equanimity and even cheerfulness. I have met scores of women, some professing Christians, and some not, who seem to sense and accept intuitively the Way of the Cross. Many wives and mothers, for example, seem to know by the light of nature that a happy home cannot be maintained and that a child cannot be trained in the way he should go without their having to bear a personal cross. But I am not at all sure that most men have the same intuitive perception of what people or situations call for in terms of personal cost, nor, as a rule, have they the same willing patience to accept it. Why, speaking generally, there should be this difference between the sexes I frankly do not know, but I do know that as people, whether men or women, come to life at the touch of the Spirit, they begin to see with the utmost clarity that the costly way of sacrifice is inevitable to the true follower of Christ. I think we do well to remember that the cheerful and willing acceptance of such a principle comes much more easily as well as more quickly to some

66

temperaments than to others. If, for example, you are by nature an idealist and you find it easier to lead than to follow, it will be a hundred times harder for you to recognize and accept what the patient Way of the Cross will mean in your own personal life. I believe this is the sort of fact which we should never forget in our thoughts and prayers about one another.

When we are young, enthusiastic and full of dreams and ideals, the skillful speaker can very readily make us feel how noble and shining is the road of self-forgetting service. But those who are swept away on a tide of youthful enthusiasm may find, even some years later, that they had no idea of the magnitude or the quality of the sacrifices which would be demanded of them. Still less did they imagine that the life of a fully committed Christian is one of continuous sacrifice, even though it of course contains its own inexpressible joys and satisfactions. All of us who are honestly committed to the Way of Christ, whether we are missionaries or not, should pause from time to time and with open eyes freely recognize exactly what sacrifices we are being called upon to make. In many of us there is much hidden resentment and rebellion—which is rarely allowed to come to the surface—which prevents us from being happy and relaxed Christians. It is commonly as we receive the broken Body and poured-out Blood of our Lord that we can cheerfully reaccept the total cost that is being demanded of us, and grasp afresh the resources which will enable us to take up our particular cross daily.

So long as there is no real acceptance of the Cross, Christian living is unnecessarily tough. The "easy yoke" and "the light burden" promised by Christ to His followers are in fact experienced only by those who in their innermost hearts accept life in His way. Here, in a small example from a hospital in Nigeria, we may see the transformation in one life from conscientious drudgery to happy service. What happened here can happen in the soul of anyone who is committed to the Way of the Cross:

"A short time ago she [the staff midwife] came to me late one night with a letter in her hand. She said she was 'ashamed' (meaning too shy) to talk. In the letter she told me that at last she thought she was beginning to understand what we meant about Christian vocation and service. We had a long talk, and she told me she had always 'tried her best' both in her work and in her personal life (which is true, for she has always been a most conscientious person), but it had always been 'hard work,' till suddenly a new spirit of joy seemed to fill her and she went on to tell how instead of work being 'duty' it was now with eagerness and with new freedom of spirit that she came to her work day by day. The change in her has been obvious to us all; she is indeed a new creature, a radiantly happy person doing the same good work but in a new way."

For most of us such a transformation of attitude comes neither quickly nor easily. Indeed, we may go on for years without realizing quite what we have undertaken in following the One whom we love. When outward circumstances are easy and there is no particular pain in being at least a superficial Christian, the implications of living under the Cross may be far from obvious. Another letter from Africa says:

". . . In fact it is respectable to be a Christian. But there *is* lack of understanding of what it means and involves, es-

68

pecially in regard to what kind of things in daily life are involved in taking up the Cross. I know it is by no means only the Africans who don't understand the connexion! I myself often fail to see it and rebel against difficulties. I think that for us the Cross should mean going on and on bearing other people, even when they don't seem to understand what being Christian means, or appear to have no standard of honesty, or after seeming to have a sense of vocation, disappoint us by complaining of overwork or asking for more money."

We have already seen something of the tragedy and embarrassment of nominal Christians. It is still in many parts of the mission field only too easy to "go through the motions" and be taken for a Christian. Yet the Cross has a strange magnetic power, and even though they be a small minority there are nearly always those who are touched by this crowning demonstration of the power of love and are inspired to give loving service in return. Here are a few sentences from Sierra Leone:

"It is the few who have learnt something of the meaning of the Cross who are really willing to go the second mile and do more than they are paid to do. We were glad to find some who are serving in this way—young men who in addition to their school work are running voluntary night schools for adults and helping with church services and we were glad to have reports of students on teaching practice who had identified themselves with the local church and helped in its activities."

It has often been said that it is petty irritations rather than great crises that wear down the human spirit. Men and women who would be magnificent when faced with danger or death find it most difficult to endure the petty frustrations of ordinary life. One aspect of the cheerful bearing of the Cross which we must never lose sight of is the unheroic, undramatic trials which must be borne with good humor. A letter from Nigeria contains these healthy words:

"Here our 'sufferings' consist chiefly of leaking roofs; a water-logged compound; safaris of biting ants; the inevitable small hurtings of one another in a small community; and the admittedly nauseating task of filling up government forms. Surely God can indeed use all these as the means of our sanctification, but I shrink from using the awe-full names of religious experience for our tuppeny-ha'penny trials. We have lots of fun and the assurance denied to so many folk, that we are doing a job that needs doing."

We at home can imagine something of the smaller crosses, but it is almost impossible for us to feel with any real sympathy what active domestic persecution might mean. We read only too easily such words of Christ as, "A man's foes shall be those of his own household," without fully realizing that that prophecy is a deadly truth today in many parts of the world. From Malaya come these words:

"Some of the girls come to the Youth service . . . some listen from outside. None of them has taken any definite step; we do not fully realize the difficulties and what pressure may be put on them in their homes and by other people in the village if they openly accept Christ. The cross they may have to live under is one we have never had to experience."

How many of us would be ready to witness bravely for Christ if it meant losing the love and indeed incurring the bitter hatred of those who are our nearest and dearest?

The Cross as a Way of Life

A correspondent from South India wonders whether the present situation is merely a lull before the storm:

"I am writing this on a friend's veranda on a Sunday morning and a more peaceful scene cannot be imagined. . . . But the question in our minds is 'How long will it last?' Are we moving towards the testing time when Christians will have to suffer for the Faith? . . . Or, are we to continue as at present outwardly peaceful, but with a slowly decreasing amount of freedom and a slowly increasing temptation to compromise?"

Even the present time of toleration for Christians has its own temptations. Again, it is not a bold dramatic stand against possible death that is being called for but a firm front to be maintained in the face of corruption and bribery. These further words come from India:

"When a Christian refuses to conform to established custom because he is a Christian, and thereby forgoes some benefit or faculty to which he is entitled, he is participating in the sufferings of Christ, and one is encouraged by the many stories one hears of Christians taking this stand. . . . This is a case where the Cross must be borne, and the whole Church should, if necessary, bear it with those who by the making of the stand forgo what they might otherwise have had."

It would appear from the many letters that I have read from India that not all Christians realize the probability of a time of suffering ahead, as perhaps these words will show:

"The Church is conscious of its need for an outpouring of the Holy Spirit, but Christians, for the most part, do not seem to realize that this will result not in pleasant emotional experience, but in a challenge to witness and a call to suffer.

A revived Church must be by nature a witnessing Church and under the present circumstances in India courageous uncompromising witness to Christ will be a costly undertaking."

The suffering has not yet come in any active form, but already there are penalties attached to the declaring of oneself as a Christian. Yet from another part come these heartening words:

"One evening a group of small boys was sitting around my feet at the door of the tent, and I asked them about their work in school. One little fellow said: 'Do you know that they want us to say we are Mahara (Scheduled Class) and not Christians?' I asked who 'they' were, and the reply came, 'Our teachers, and they say it will be to our advantage to put ourselves down as Scheduled Class.' I then asked what they had done and like lightning came the reply, 'Why, of course we put our names down as Christians. Isn't that our right? Don't we believe in Jesus Christ, so how can we put ourselves down as Hindus?' Yes! how can they? And yet some of them do, for it takes courage to call oneself a Christian when one can benefit by not doing so, especially when one is poor and downtrodden. . . .

"There are scholarships, and all sorts of privileges for children of the Scheduled Classes from which children of Christians are debarred. Yes! it takes courage to be a Christian in India to-day, yet there is no open persecution."

The need is plainly for courage and faithfulness, and there is a subtle, unrelenting temptation not to declare oneself too openly as a Christian.

Quite apart from the cross involved in facing active or hidden persecution, there is always in Christian living the cross of sacrifice. It is not easy to give when it is to our apparent considerable impoverishment, but here in a letter from South India comes an illuminating glimpse of the spirit of sacrifice. The sacrifice is not one of money but of something much more valuable: of trained people. Yet this diocese is ready to make the sacrifice and has already grasped the truth of the Christian paradox that the more we give, the more we receive:

"When we ourselves are in need of more pastors, it may be asked whether we are justified in giving up the services of these promising men to work in other lands; I really believe this is a step in the right direction. We have already sent ministers to look after large congregations of people from this diocese who reside in the cities of Calcutta, Bombay, Bangalore and Madras. I believe all this is to our advantage and spiritual growth. The more we give out of our best, the greater will be our blessings."

But it is easy not to make the sacrifice, and we all know how ready we are to find reasons for our choices when we know in our heart of hearts that personal gain and the evasion of the Cross are our real motives. Only those who have really embraced the way of the Cross can stand against the temptation to evade. From Ruanda comes this message:

"Some of the churches near the Tanganyika border are being severely tested in these days. Numbers of teachers are going off to Uganda to get money and are leaving their congregations. The temptation is very great, and only those who are really saved, and are willing to trust the Lord, are able to stand."

Yet another message from the same area shows the pattern we have observed before, that there are always some who are prepared to accept the hard way of the Cross:

"During this last year, those we have witnessed going on with the Lord have been those who have been willing, very often, to stand alone from the general stream, those who in some cases have had to be willing to lose friends, money and many other things for Jesus' sake. Praise the Lord for those who have been willing to pay the price, and walk the way of the Cross."

But bearing the Cross does not always mean refusing to compromise with evil nor making sacrifice, nor refusing to take the easy path. Sometimes it simply means gay and patient endurance of physical suffering, the winning of an intimate personal battle by the power of the Cross. From a hospital in the Upper Nile Diocese an observer can write these words:

"When we see the quite amazing cheerfulness with which so many of our patients cope with the really horrible deformities and ulcers that so many of the late cases have; with what patience they face what they know means years of treatment—more than patience, courage and gaiety too—we stand at the foot of the Cross and wonder and give praise. With that in front of us, how can we do anything less than our utmost to take our share of the weight of the Cross?"

There seems almost no end to the variety of crosses which the Christian may be called upon to bear. But the essential principle remains the same—that if he accepts his particular cross with a good heart God is able to turn the evil in the situation into a positive power for good.

Quite frequently, as I think we have already noticed, the sacrifice required is one of pride and position. But it is only fair to add that it is quite possible for people to go on unconsciously for years in a "superior" position. In Sierra Leone, for example, in the early days the Gospel was preached mainly to the Creoles, and this gave them additional reason for being a "superior" people. Now the Cross is appearing in that situation and it is apparent that if the thousands of people who are not Creoles are to be won for Christ, Christians must be prepared to abandon any position of privilege.

Sometimes the bearing of the Cross is very far from being a matter of static patient faithfulness. The call is to high adventure requiring vision, courage and initiative and the willingness to bear any variety of suffering under the Cross. The annals of missionary enterprise are full of such real crusading, but not all the thrilling tales belong to the past. To take only one example of modern pioneering, there is the story of a missionary in Pakistan. This gay and dauntless woman led eighteen families out into the desert to make a new home for them under the Government Resettlement Scheme. In frightful heat, with every possible shortage of supplies, with barely enough water to sustain life, these Christians have labored together to build their village. The promised canals have not yet materialized and the surrounding desert remains scorched and barren, yet their hearts are high. The end of their story has still to be written, but here is a contemporary cross being bravely borne.

I have left till last, because I am sure the Christians concerned would leave it till last—if they ever spoke of it—the particular cross of being a lonely Christian. We may think of a missionary who is far from home and familiar things, of his daily burden of anxieties and frustrations and of his temptation at times to utter despair. But at least the European missionary knows that behind him stands the prayer and moral support of his Society. He may look forward to furloughs, proper attention and care if he is sick, and an honorable retirement when his work is done. I hope that we who are missionary supporters at home never forget these lonely brothers and sisters in the Gospel. But do we not sometimes all too readily forget the cross which falls upon the lonely Christian national bravely witnessing for Christ among his own people? We need to remember the pastors, the catechists, the teachers, as well as the hosts of ordinary men and women who, humanly speaking, have no one to support them. Ideally, of course, the whole Church is behind them, but in practice this must indeed be difficult for many a Christian national to feel. He has made, and usually goes on making, great sacrifices to become and remain a Christian at all. He is always in a minority, frequently in a minority of one. It is not the least of the miracles of the Gospel that such people maintain their bright and cheerful witness day in and day out without respite and with almost every possible discouragement. They, equally with our European brothers and sisters, should claim our love and our prayer. Their cross of isolation, of being cut off from the customs and ways of thinking of the nation in which they were born, is a heavy one indeed.

Do we try to appreciate fully the courage and faithfulness of isolated Christian nationals as well as of those men and women who do not merely "take an interest" in the worldwide Church, but go out personally to serve it? How many of us at home in our comparative ease and comfort could bear the loneliness, the drudgery and the often overt presence of evil day after day for years on end? Surely the least we can do is to support our "front line troops" by every means at our disposal—certainly not least by earnest, sympathetic intercession for them.

VII

The Cross in Frustration and Tragedy

In a world which worships above all things success, efficiency and results, one of the most difficult and heartbreaking crosses we may be called upon to bear is that of an isolated and apparently fruitless witness. I have so often heard shallow-minded people say that if only Christ is faithfully proclaimed and His Cross faithfully uplifted there are bound to be conversions by the score or even by the thousand. Of course, that is not true, and if such people were better informed about the apparently fruitless work of the Church of Christ in the tough parts of the world they would not talk such arrant nonsense. For the evangelist at home there may be a big organization, a plentiful supply of money, the assistance of trained counselors, many of the resources of modern science to amplify his efforts—and no persecution worth mentioning. The evangelist overseas, whether foreigner or national of the country, has none of these things; and against him in his

loneliness there are often ranged centuries of prejudice, ignorance and apathy.

In every kind of Christian work there is a certain casting
of bread upon the waters and a sowing of seed which, if it
grows at all, grows secretly. But on the Christian in a really
difficult area, who year after year sees no result for all his
faithful witness, this particular aspect of the Cross must bear
almost intolerably. All Christians who are doing the work of
Christ in trying to extend His Kingdom know disappointment,
frustration and failure, but most of them know of success, of
joyful surprises, of unexpected spiritual quickenings, which
they can set off in their minds against the heartbreaks. But
suppose the daily round is one of faithful witness but of apparently unremitting failure? To what temptations of utter
despair—even of radical doubt of the power and validity of
the Gospel itself—must such people be exposed!

For myself one of the greatest impressions ever made upon
me in my student days was made by a missionary returned
from the Yukon, who labored and prayed for fifteen years before he saw a single conversion. Men and women work
patiently and faithfully under appalling discouragement, and
the continual temptation to surrender should not only call
forth our admiration but evoke our most earnest prayers. Yet
in a sense they are called to live very near Christ and His
Cross, for was there ever such an apparent failure as Calvary?

It is all very well for us who are on the safe side of that
ghastly tragedy, when evil men put out the Light, to see the
Cross as a triumph. At the time when it happened surely it
must have appeared to be the very end of the world, even to
those who loved Jesus best. The early promise was blighted,
the wonderful teaching proved to be powerless in the face of

78

evil, the promised Kingdom a mere dream, when the King Himself was shown to be as mortal as any man. No wonder we read that when the inevitable end became apparent "they all forsook him and fled." Yet, from our own safe point of view we know that the failure and weakness, final and appalling as they appeared, were only the prelude to the most resounding triumph that the world has ever seen. "He was crucified in weakness," wrote St. Paul, *"but He was raised in power."* Indeed, it was but a very short time before the hated and dreaded Cross, the very symbol of public humiliating death, became the sign in which the Church went forward to conquer.

There are undoubtedly those who are called to bear faithful but apparently fruitless witness in the dark places of the earth. They have to be very sure of God's Will for them, and sometimes their only consolation is that they are very near our Lord Himself in His loneliness, desolation and agony. But if they are so called they may also know that the deepest of all tragedies became the most resplendent of all triumphs. As far as this little life is concerned they may not see even so much as the seed sprouting. Yet they will most certainly one day know the truth of the words: "They that sow in tears shall reap in joy."

Although in reading scores of letters and reports from overseas I have come across no hint of querulousness or self-pitying, it is quite plain that many in quite unconscious heroism are bearing a cross with apparently very little result. Here, for example, is part of a letter from one difficult area in Africa:

". . . Although the definite *shadow* of the Cross of Christ is upon this land, that shadow is upon it in much the same way as the shadow of Calvary fell on the hardened Pharisee, the worldly soldier, the jeering spectator; they were 'Under the Cross' all right, but not in the same sense as St. Peter and the others, nor as interpreted in the more specifically 'revival' areas of the mission field. I hope I'm not being too pessimistic about this, but our chapter is a grim one in these days."

From a Moslem area in another part of Africa we read:

"So little has been the impact of Christianity on the Moslems that they do not oppose missionary work among them because they fear no success on the part of the Christians. This is a Moslem stronghold but the Moslems welcome our going here to bring any help we can. I don't think they fear any conversions!"

And here I quote from a letter from yet another Moslem area:

"If we cannot be a pioneer school showing new ideas and new freedom in education, and if in the sphere of religion we are so harmless and inoffensive to the Moslems that they are not afraid of us, what is the purpose of having a C.M.S. school here? Nearly seven-eighths of our girls are Moslems, and they all attend prayers and scripture lessons, but it is fairly certain that parents would not send their girls to us if they thought that there was any danger of their being converted to Christianity. We must not overlook the importance of the seed growing secretly, so long as it is growing."

These extracts point to some of the questions which are bound to arise in the mind of any Christian, whatever his race, who is concerned with the spread of the Gospel but finds himself in a situation in which there appears to be no spiritual response: "Is it worth while for me to stay here? Am I still sure I am in the place God wants me to be? Is this one of the cases where we are to 'shake the dust off our feet' and move on to an area where they are hungry for the Gospel?" And then, as materialism and "education" press blindly but irresistibly forward, the tiny Church is powerless and God Himself appears to do nothing, even more searching questions must arise: "Why has God sent me here merely to feel impotent, frustrated and heartbroken? Is God deaf to our prayers and entreaties? Does He remain indifferent to the fate of the souls of these people?"

Even the little that such Christians have succeeded in building is in these days often in danger of being swept away. How hard, how desperately hard for those who are called to work here to "strengthen the things that remain"—and how desperately easy to lose faith!

For those of us not in such a situation there is surely a trumpet call to join the army of intercessors. For in the mysterious fellowship of intercessory prayer we can be reliable allies of some of these lonely but undaunted fellow Christians in other lands.

When we were children one of our sharpest pains was the pain of disappointment. Even when we are grown up and are making some headway toward Christian maturity, disappointment, although somewhat of a different kind, can very nearly break our hearts. It is not now the denial of our own wishes but the failure of those whom we have loved and served, for whom we have worked and prayed, that can disappoint us so poignantly. Here is an extract from a letter from Western India:

"Even those who have gone ahead and responded to teaching have also much to learn. This year I have seen one of our men drag his wife by her hair across a yard with her nine-year-old daughter clinging to her; I have housed all day on two different occasions women who have been unmercifully beaten by their so-called Christian husbands. I have seen Christians resort to magic as a cure for snake-bite . . . here we are in the midst of the struggle, encouraged to go on only because we know that the battle is the Lord's. . . . Pray especially . . . that this awful backsliding may be checked, as truly the last stage is far worse than when they were Hindus."

Failures and backslidings call for more than human patience, patience that is rooted in the boundless love of the Cross. Without this divine resource we very quickly grow impatient, despairing or resentful. From Dornakal, from a school in a "mass movement" area come these words written in the midst of a very busy life:

"The important task in all such work is to try to form Christian character and it is with this aim that we must work. The title of this year's letter 'Under the Cross' sounds very heroic, and I don't feel that this work is heroic. But we do know that the children with whom we deal daily, in garden and kitchen and schoolroom and Cathedral, are children for whom Christ died and for whose allegiance He longs, and it is surely worth all the weariness of routine of school and hostel work, if in some small way one can have the privilege of bringing these children nearer to Christ, built up in His likeness into the service of His Church."

"It doesn't sound very heroic," says the writer, and indeed, here is no battle with open evil, no faithful stand against persecution, in fact nothing dramatic at all. But is there no heroism in coping daily with wearying routine, with the never ending demands of growing personalities and with the constant temptation to forget quality in the presence of overwhelming quantity?

The same temptation to be defeated by time and rush, to allow the superficial to master the real, is evident from another letter, this time from West Africa:

"In spite of a heavy time-table and many other attractions one would always find staff and students taking their places in chapel, some time before the bell was rung. I believe lives are truly consecrated and promises faithfully made during these times but the 'pull' in the towns and villages, from those who are not convinced of the Truth, is so great that we do have big disappointments. It appears that book-knowledge demands all the attention, while training for 'life' is the concern of a very small number of people.

"We wish more men would give thought to the planning of a Christian home, but there seems little time for such things. We become so immersed in all that is demanded of us from central organizations that we lose sight of our vision and calling."

The painful and sometimes unbearable difference between vision and practical reality, between what we should like to see happen and what actually does happen, is probably common to us all. Here in the Church at home over a period of years we have grown accustomed to certain compromises; we have grown to accept the fact that certain things can, and certain things cannot, be done. We know frustration but not as it is felt by the eager Christian who loves the people among whom he works and upon whose scene there have come with frightening suddenness irreversible developments and expansions. So much to be done, and so little he can do!

These words from Uganda might well have come from any fast-developing area. Let us read them as representative of something of the frustrations felt by those who would do so much but can in fact do so little:

"The particular, persistent and unrelieved quality which has coloured our work during the past year has been frustration. This probably is not a bad thing in connexion with . . . the theme 'Under the Cross' as frustration teaches many lessons.

"It has often been said that people matter more than things. The tragedy of this programme of expansion is that, so often, inevitably, during the growing pains, it is the people who suffer. Sometimes it is suggested that everything should close down and there should be no intake during the following year. . . .

"This annual letter must be one that records disappointments; the year has seen high hopes deflated. . . .

"Briefly, the difference between the Christian and the secular outlook on the educational work out here is that, to the Christian, education is only worthy when it is centred in a life dedicated to Christ; whereas to the secular man education is an end in itself, which breeds freely all graces and benefits to the civilized state.

"Nothing worries me more than to hear—as I often hear even the staff of this college say: We are really only 'Government under another name.' This is not true; but indeed it only could be true if that other Name were truly Christ, and under His Name we stand and try."

A Christian who teaches the Love and Providence of God is bound, whether he likes it or not, to "vindicate the ways of God to man." Every Christian indeed, even in this country, has at some time or another to attempt to do the same before his unbelieving friends. But how infinitely harder such a task must be when the welfare and even survival of hundreds of thousands of people depend upon what appear to be the whims of nature! Let us read with imagination these words from the Bombay Diocese:

"One further matter must be mentioned—that of the monsoon, for it affects everything. A good monsoon means enough to eat for the year and sometimes a small margin over which allows the purchase of a bullock or buffalo or to build a new mud-house or deepen a well. For the lonely leader of the local church it means being practically cut off . . . rivers rise, roads are closed, transport stops. Failure of the monsoon is a catastrophe. We face that again this year. We've had showers, but not the downpour expected and needed. Maize sown with the first showers is fast drying up. There is no fodder for the cattle. Everywhere special prayers are being said. Here sixty to seventy folk have met every morning at dawn for prayer for rain and seek God's blessing on their families, homes and crops. 'We believe God will hear our prayers and send the rain,' they say, 'but if not—we are still His children and He will care for us.' "

Would you, would I, care to have to explain the ways of God to simple people to whom the coming of sufficient rain means all the difference between prosperity and near starvation? Even to attempt any kind of explanation means the Cross in our heads as well as in our hearts.

In our own comparatively safe country any untoward natural incident is referred to in our insurance policies as "an act of God," but who would dare give this name to the recent fearful disaster in the Punjab? Twelve thousand square miles were inundated in Pakistan, crops were ruined, cattle drowned and buildings damaged or destroyed on a vast scale. Simultaneously from the same cause in India, 175,000 houses collapsed and it is known at the moment of writing that at least 7,000 villages have suffered. Of course, it could be argued that had there been better relations between India and Pakistan the normal river and canal services on both sides of the frontier would by now have been better organized and a flood of such tragic dimensions might have been averted. This is debatable. It is known that the engineers concerned on both sides of the frontier did their best in the circumstances. But whatever man might have done, the fact remains that "unprecedented rains" overwhelmed the whole complicated water system.

If Christians were not able to explain or vindicate the disaster they turned without delay to mitigate it. Here are a few words from Amritsar:

"Many thousands have lost their homes and all they possess. Many are still surrounded by water and cut off from everything. Our Bishop and his helpers are going out day by day with clothes, blankets and medicines, strengthening and helping the people in the Name of Jesus. We have collected hundreds of clothes for the refugees, for the cold weather is beginning."

In the face of such widespread disaster pre-Christian memories not unnaturally began to stir. "The gods of the rivers are laughing. Men from the cities dam them and drain them into straight lines—their canals—yet the gods of the five rivers are strong. They break their chains and laugh. . . ." Then came the Christian voice: "But no! There are no gods but God, and He is good." And another voice added, "And

He let His own Son suffer too." We read that an Indian Christian doing his best to help in the disaster "was greeted by a group of Christian matrons and young girls balancing petrol tins full of water on their heads. They were returning from one of the few wells which had not been inundated and polluted. It had been a long walk.

"No stranger would have guessed as the women passed in single file—their faces serene, their tongues perhaps unusually inactive—that they had lost everything which means 'home' to a woman the world over—their brass and tin cups and plates, their bits of furniture, the gaily-patterned quilt so essential when the Punjab 'cold weather' gets going, odds and ends picked up for a few annas at a Christmas *mela* (fair), their Sunday-best saris, the cheap but venerated prints of Bible stories that adorned their walls."

As soon as coherent news of this flood disaster was available, the *C.M.S. News* published a report. Here is part of it:

" 'We have lost five churches and five catechists' houses. This is the third flood in this area in five years, and it is hard for the people to bear. In all, sixty villages with Christian congregations have been seriously affected, at least twenty-eight Christians have lost their lives and a large number are destitute.

" 'Church buildings have been completely swept away in some places. Catechists have no place to go for shelter and their clothes, food stores and other possessions are buried under the debris and will be useless even if dug up.'

"On receipt of these and other reports the C.M.S. Committee decided to increase its grants this year to affected areas by $14,000, and in spite of all other commitments to make as much as necessary of this sum available at once."

It is easy from the appearance of things to say that there can be no God to permit such disasters, or to despair in face of the sheer size of the catastrophe. But the Christian can and does trust where he cannot understand, and he meets the evil of disaster by doing everything within his power to ease the vast burden of suffering. Even for us to sit quietly and contemplate actually having to live through such a situation as our brothers and sisters have lived through in India and Pakistan will bring home to us something of this particular cross, the bearing of apparently pointless and undeserved suffering.

There are crosses of bitter disappointment and agonizing frustration on the "home front" as well. I want to mention here two types of people who are a real part of the total picture, but who can be all too readily forgotten.

First, let us spend a little kindly thought for the missionary recruit who for some good reason or another is not accepted for service. From his own point of view the vision which has led him on for years, which may have taught him to endure hardship and sacrifice, and has finally brought him to offer himself for wholly dedicated service, leads in the end to nothing more than a kindly but firm refusal. For him the skies are dark indeed. It is hard for him not to feel he has been cruelly deceived as well as tragically mistaken.

This particular cross is by no means wholly borne by the recruit himself. Those who interview him in the full flush of his genuine enthusiasm and sense of vocation are humbly grateful for his offer, and it is sometimes extremely painful to turn down such eagerness and devotion. But what the recruit cannot know in any detail is the actual situation in

Africa and Asia. Today that situation is a more searching test of men and women from this country than it has ever been before. Those who have to bear the heavy responsibility of deciding whether or not to accept a man or woman have to consider most carefully the factors of health, temperament, experience and qualifications. In many cases, after balanced consideration, they feel reluctantly compelled to say that they cannot accept a particular recruit. But it can hardly be emphasized too strongly that this does not mean rejection from God's service, or that the sense of a call to that service has been mistaken. With the utmost gentleness and love we may have to point out that it is, rather, a misunderstanding of the particular field of work to which He was calling them. God calls no man to make a fool of him, but He can and does call men to bear crosses. Here the particular cross may be the cheerful acceptance of the unpalatable—that for some reason or other, quite probably through no fault of his own, missionary service abroad is not the work for him.

But service here at home, the building up of the Church of God, the strengthening of the home front of the world-wide work of the Church—in these fields there are dozens of tasks crying out for men and women to undertake them. If God has truly called us we may be quite certain that he has a place for us in the world-wide economy of His Church. As for those of us who have found the work that God wants us to do, let us not forget in our prayers and thoughts those for whom the cross of disappointment is black and heavy indeed.

Secondly, I am sure we should spare a great deal more than a passing thought for those devoted hard-working and often lonely souls who keep the flag of missionary interest flying in literally hundreds of parishes in our land. A great many congregations are thoroughly parochially-minded, and through sheer lack of vision the work of the world-wide Church is frequently regarded as a nuisance, a Cinderella, or a poor relation. In some parishes to my certain knowledge the real glory of the vast task throughout the world is seen by very few, perhaps even by only one solitary missionary secretary. God alone knows what crosses of disappointment and frustration such folk have to bear. The incumbent may be too busy for them, and the people may even regard them as a little queer in their lonely enthusiasm for missionary work. Yet to them has been given the vision, and to their unflagging loyalty and steadfastness we owe the fact that the cause of the world-wide Church is not allowed to be forgotten. Jesus Himself prophesied strange reversals in the world of Reality to which we are bound. "Many that are first shall be last, and last first," He said. I for one should not be surprised to see a number of inconspicuous missionary secretaries wearing dazzling crowns of glory when the books are opened! In the meantime there is, if we think about it, quite a lot we can do to lighten the crosses they so uncomplainingly bear.

VIII

The Real Cross and a Manufactured Cross

SOME WEEKS ago I wrote to a shrewd Christian friend of mine in New York asking his opinion about a book with a religious flavor which was selling by the hundred thousand in the United States of America. In his reply my friend said something like this: "Part of the appeal of the book lies in the fact that the author has substituted a plastic cross for the heavy wooden one which the Good Lord sometimes calls upon us to bear." I found that reply not only amusing but very illuminating, for, human nature being what it is, we are all apt to evade the particular cross which God calls us to bear and then, to satisfy our consciences, invent a plastic one which looks impressive but is in fact perfectly comfortable to carry. On the other hand there are those who enjoy "being martyrs," as we used to say when we were children. They find it difficult to receive joy by relaxation, encouragement or praise, and are suspicious of any Christian living which is not painful and difficult. They too are manufacturing a cross, but theirs is heavier than the one God intended them to bear, and though it may bring them inward satisfaction it may rob their witness of Christian gaiety and inner relaxation.

The plain fact is that the Christian must accept life at the hands of his Father. If he is called to pain, distress or persecution he must be free from resentment; if he is called to times of joy and satisfaction he must not go around looking for the "snags"—he must accept thankfully every happiness from the hands of Him who gives us "richly all things to enjoy." In short he must learn to do what St. Paul learned to do when he wrote: "I know how to be abased, and I know how to abound: everywhere and in all things I am instructed both to be full and to be hungry, both to abound and to suffer need." It seems to me that one of the most important qualities for Christian living is that of flexibility to the leading of the Spirit. Some of us have to learn to accept joyfully disappointments and frustrations—as they seem to us. Others of us have to learn that it may be God's Will to abandon our painful and heroic labors, secretly satisfying though they are, and with equal cheerfulness accept happier and more congenial work. The all-important thing is to follow the leading of the Spirit.

Now it seems important to me to point out here what sometimes seems to us an arbitrariness in the leading of the Spirit. No doubt we remember the occasion when St. Paul "assayed to go into Bithynia," but St. Luke simply records that "the Spirit suffered them not." Did God then not love the people of Bithynia? Did He not will them to hear the everlasting Gospel? Why should it be more important for the people of Macedonia to hear the Gospel than for the pagans of Bithynia? The answer is simply that we do not know, but it raises in our minds the whole question of this apparent arbitrariness of God. We can put the question further back and ask, Why should the Jews have received God's Law and Promise while the Romans and Egyptians, for example, apparently received so little revelation from His hand? We might similarly ask, Why should the South American Indians or the inhabitants of Central Africa be left for century after century in the most appalling darkness of spirit? If we pursue such a question we find no answer at all. Although we know and are convinced that God "willeth all men to be saved," our finite minds simply cannot understand God's apparent "neglect" of millions of His own creatures. Obviously some of the failure to spread the Good News since the days of Christ must be laid squarely at the door of an apathetic, timid and indolent Church. But this is far from being a complete answer, and we are forced to conclude that in following the leading of the Spirit we are following a plan which we can only partially understand. I don't suppose that St. Paul broke his heart over the apparently "neglected" people of Bithynia: he was far too set on following a Wisdom higher than his own. Similarly, as the world-wide Church moves forward into new positions, it has got to accept many apparent "neglects" and not be anxious about them.

In my younger days I must confess that to "burn out for God" sounded to me not only noble and romantic, but the highest form of Christian service. Now I am quite sure it is not; I have become convinced that it is our job as "servants of the Lord" to burn brightly and clearly for as long as possible

THE CHURCH UNDER THE CROSS

and not indulge in any self-pleasing heroics. It is the real Cross that we must bear, and not one of self-dramatization. Here are some sane words from a doctor overseas:

"I am more than ever convinced that people can't work together unless they can play together as well as pray together. We have instituted a compulsory frivol once a month and every Wednesday evening has to be kept free of station work, so that anyone who wants to, can either foregather or go off on their own devices. Another thing we try to insist on as far as possible, is a regular week-end off, preferably away from the station. . . . It is easy in this sort of life to drive oneself too hard for efficiency. I discovered this myself the hard way about ten years ago as a country G.P. It was during the war and I was trying to run a double practice single-handed. I started to get increasingly proud of the number of hours I was putting in each day, and quite failed to recognize that the standard of my work was falling off. . . . The result was that I cracked rather completely and had to take three months off. I have heard of several similar instances in work overseas, and, after a year out here I can see the danger is even greater than it was [at home]."

One of my favorite sentences in the New Testament is from St. John 4. 6: "Jesus therefore, being wearied with his journey, sat thus on the well." I have met so many high-pressure Christians in my time who would certainly never have allowed anybody to sit down in the middle of a ministry as important as that of Jesus! We do well to remember that if Jesus had not taken a few minutes off for relaxation He would not have had the conversation with the woman at the well. In the letters of several missionaries it is obvious that a "conscience" urging them to be hard at it all the time is in conflict with common sense which suggests that a more relaxed way of living may not only be more pleasant but even more fruitful. Here are some sensible words from a letter from Nigeria:

"Another thing I've learnt here is the importance of the apparently unimportant. Maybe we do not think very much of omitting to greet someone in the morning or of uttering a hasty word in a moment of annoyance. But these things can mean a lot. Not very long ago my houseboy's small sisters came to visit him. It is my custom to greet his relations or friends when they come to the house, but on this occasion, for some reason or other I did not do this. The result was that those small children went home at once because they thought I was angry with them. . . .

"Three days ago I was helping with a Federal by-election. During a break in the voting I got out my food, and because I feel embarrassed if I am the only one eating, I offered some to the policeman, my polling officer and the party agents. I also got into conversation with the policeman, during the course of which he said that I was the kindest European he'd ever met. I don't say this to get any credit for myself, but just to illustrate that it is often the small and apparently unimportant thing which has the greatest effect."

We are all familiar with the truism that "people are more important than things." For myself as I study the remarkable poise of Jesus in the Gospel stories, it appears to me that people are also more important to Him than time. Certainly it seems to me that for the follower of Jesus actual contacts with people must never be crowded out by any preconceived schedule, however praiseworthy and important the keeping of it may seem. If once we let the schedule, the scheme, the plan, or even the routine become our master it will not be long before the job becomes more important to us than the people whom the job is designed to serve. These words from East Africa are typical of many letters from different parts of the mission field:

"The barriers to real meeting with people are those of insufficient time for one's ordinary jobs and teaching, leaving little just to chat with girls or staff; tiredness which makes one disinclined to make the effort to meet with others; and the barrier of language increased by the fact that we teach in English, and have little time or opportunity for practising Luganda. . . ."

That the times of off-duty are important is apparent to many missionaries. Fun and games have a real part to play in maintaining balanced and effective life. From Wusasa in Nigeria come these words:

"All work and no play makes Jack a dull boy. Here, as in any other place, it is important to have outside social contacts and we do value these both for what we can receive and what we can give. The Christmas parties for European children brought out all the children within a radius of sixteen miles and a host of parents from every walk of life open to Europeans in this land. They were a tremendous source of contact. Father Christmas came riding on the Emir's camel to the great delight of both young and old."

Of course, it is not easy to plan our lives when we are thousands of miles away from a familiar pattern of living which plans our time for us. Here are some frank and revealing words from a nurse in Pakistan: the problem she is facing is faced in some degree by all who are working on the thinly held front line of the Church in action:

"A great deal is said about sacrifice on the mission field,

meaning a severance from the opportunity of making money, from realizing an ambition, from family and friends, home ties, and our recognized standard of living. I don't agree. . . . I think that the greatest sacrifice is that of personality. Perhaps the thing I have found most noticeable along these lines on my return after almost a year in my former job of nursing at home was the ease of mind one had there in relation to one's work and leisure. To be able to find beauty and self-expression in complicated embroidery, or hours of gardening, listening to a radio programme of good music, reading, enjoying one's nephews and family and friends, knowing that one had complied with all the requirements in regard to one's work and that one was not 'stealing' time—this was indeed a peace of mind I valued. How difficult to reconcile this matter out here in our haphazard living, for try how we will, we do not seem to be able to make it otherwise. It is easier to give in than fight it out again and again with one's conscience, so many of us feel. . . . Does it mean deeper consecration? Does it mean more common sense?"

We all need to remember how Jesus Himself lived. Sermons are preached on the recorded fact that Jesus got up early in the morning for prayer, but I for one have yet to hear a sermon preached on the same Jesus' insistence on withdrawal, indeed retreat, from the crowds who were needing Him so much, or on how He was not ashamed to fall deeply asleep aboard a small boat and leave the bailing of the boat to His friends. Again, we need to remember that Jesus did not apparently feel it in any way a waste of time to attend a wedding feast or accept other social invitations, even from the disreputable. He was not always preaching, healing and teaching. That He enjoyed ordinary social life was probably the reason for His enemies' accusation that He was a gluttonous man and a winebibber. If Jesus is our Pattern, social contacts are as necessary to healthy living as prayer itself. Many missionaries realize this, as these few words from Kenya will show:

"The African headmaster of the local Intermediate School and his wife are very friendly. We were there for dinner the other day and they have been to us. As we came away the other night, the wife said: 'Oh! I wish you were coming again tomorrow night.' We realized as we had not done before that they are *lonely* and starved of the kind of companionship they have both had in training. It is desperately difficult to find time for friends whether black or white—and in the end there is nothing more necessary . . . there are also those men who are now out in country districts with little to occupy them except the job, who need friendship, some social life and, most of them, Christian fellowship of rather a different pattern from that provided by the Revival."

Personally I find the closing words rather significant. Most normal people need ordinary human social contact to keep them healthy in mind. As I study the Figure of matchless stature and quality who walks so surely through the pages of the Gospels I do not find it difficult to imagine Him enjoying both the dinner party of Zaccheus and an evening spent in quiet friendship with Mary, Martha and Lazarus. The tempo of Christ's life was never hectically hurried despite its superhuman responsibility, and I think all of us would do well to study His poise and balance.

Necessary as social contacts are, there are naturally times when we must, as He did, get away from people altogether and leave the work to look after itself. From India a missionary writes of this need, and as we read these words we should remember that the need of the Asian—or African—pastor is every whit as great:

". . . I am sure that every missionary ought to make a retreat once a year. It may be asked: 'What will happen to the work?' Retreats, times of withdrawal are so important that three or four days of the annual holiday might well be set aside . . . for each missionary to take part in a retreat somewhere.

"Together with this need for special retreat I feel that we ought to be stressing more the value of silence generally. Before I came to India I had the impression that this was a quiet unhurried country. In a few respects I can see that this is true, but I find that very largely there is as much noise and bustle as in the West and so there is a pressing need to conserve those precious moments of silence which are so few. We need to remember it more in our worship where, I feel, the Quakers have something to teach us."

Recently, during a visit to the United States of America, I myself felt how much Christians today need these deliberate times of retreat and silence. Much as I admired the fervor and enthusiasm of the Californian Christians to whom it was my privilege to minister, their lives almost without exception lacked, not prayer, but silence and quiet. The warmly enthusiastic prayer meeting is no substitute at all for the silence in which God can speak, and indeed in which He may teach us to relax, and not to exaggerate our own importance or responsibilities.

Each one of us has his own proper cross to bear, and it is very important that we should carry what God Himself has designed for us to bear and not what any other strong personality or pressure group would attempt to impose upon us. It is not, to my mind, the function of one particular Christian group to impose its pattern of living and worship upon another. These words from East Africa make rather disquieting reading:

"Soon after our arrival here a pastor in the town asked me if I were saved. Receiving an affirmative reply, he went on to say that there are two types of future possible for a recruit arriving here now. 'Either you come into the fellowship with us, and are blessed and used by God; or, like most Englishmen, you hold back and thereby miss the blessing.'"

Jesus Himself was in the highest degree unpopular with the "holy" and "righteous" ones of His day, but He went on steadily bearing the particular cross which He accepted from the hands of the Father. I do not know the mission field at first hand at all, but twenty-five years' experience in this country has shown me how people can be made thoroughly miserable or even driven into "breakdowns" in trying to bear crosses put upon them by others. Just as we have no excuse for evading the particular cross which God has designed for us to bear, so we have no right at all to place on other people's shoulders a cross which we think they ought to bear! At any given time our "crosses" may vary enormously; God may be simultaneously handing to one a period of severe testing and persecution and to another a period of peaceful consolidation. Christian life is like that—we must learn to accept the lighter cross as well as the heavier cross, the time of joy and peace as well as the time of pain and tribulation, with equal cheerfulness and thankfulness. Above all, we must not try to assess the weight of one another's crosses. "What is that to thee? Follow thou me." These words of Jesus to St. Peter should never be far from our recollection. What appears right for one may be quite wrong for another; what is appropriate to one area may be quite ineffective in another.

The brave bearing of particularly difficult crosses may humble us, may rebuke our own grumblings and inspire us to deeper devotion to our Lord. But it still does not follow that God is requiring us to bear, except of course in love, sympathy and intercession, the especially heavy crosses that others have to bear. How well we can sympathize with these words written by a missionary's wife at an African Leprosy Center!

"I know that at Kumi the children are facing long years of treatment, many of them a long way from their own people and tribe, but many small things cheer children and there are happy little faces everywhere. At Ongino, the adult settlement nearby, there are terribly disfigured, crippled, destitute people, some of them incapable of any work to keep them occupied, and the sheer courage with which they deal with their lives is something that almost shatters one. Leading a Bible study or Fellowship group there is a very moving and humbling experience. As my husband said when he got back last week, 'Who are we to talk to them about the Cross?'"

If we are moved at such things, how much more is the Lord of Love moved? But no good purpose is served by imagining ourselves having to bear other people's crosses, unless it lends love and sympathy to our prayers for them. Let us be quite sure of the cross which God requires each one of us to carry, and let us bear it with cheerfulness, common sense and courage.

IX

The Cross the Way of
Ultimate Victory

THE ENEMIES of Christianity sometimes think that the Christian's inner peace is due simply to the fact that the Christian has convinced himself that he is on the winning side. Of course, the Christian does feel and know that he is on the winning side, but not in the least in the sense that he has his seat for Heaven safely booked and the rest of the world can "go hang." His satisfaction and central poise arise from his conviction that the way of love, which is the way of the Cross, is the only way of ultimate victory. He himself is personally committed to such a way of living and the more he experiences it, the deeper grows his certainty that there is no other way of redeeming men, situations and, in the end, the world. He knows all about the apparent weakness of the way of love and the apparent strength of the ways of force, money and "success." But quite apart from contemporary observation, twenty centuries of history are not without their value, and the world can offer no evidence whatsoever that people are ever changed radically by anything less than the power of love.

The vastness of the task of changing people by the patient painful ways of love may frequently appal us. But once we are convinced that the moving Spirit behind the whole observable universe (and, for all we know, a million others as well) is the Spirit of self-giving, redeeming Love, we can rest our full weight of confidence upon God. We can trust where we cannot understand; we can safely leave the unsolved problems, even the perplexing "neglects" mentioned in the previous chapter, in utterly trustworthy Hands. Meanwhile, with alertness, vigor and flexibility, and all the time with the inner satisfaction that we are working on the right lines, it is our job to cooperate with the God-sized project as far as our vision and abilities allow.

Now no one, however willing and able, gets very far in this high task of cooperation with God Himself without meeting with the Cross in one or more of its many aspects. In the preceding pages I have tried to give some sort of "documentary" account of how men and women, who are trained and dedicated to the special work of the Church's front-line battles, are meeting the Cross in different ways. I have also tried, all too sketchily I am afraid, to indicate something of the vitality of the Younger Churches and of the multitudinous perils which beset them. But now I think it is time that we took a good look at ourselves, not merely to see how we can help such admirable people, but to ask a much more penetrating question—*How far are our lives being lived under the Cross?* Sometimes, in unconscious arrogance, we white-skinned people secretly think ourselves rather unusually Chris-

tian in lending our interest and our time to consider the work
of the Church overseas. We may not realize for a moment
that those whom we condescend to support may be living
lives far more genuinely under the Cross than our own lives
have ever been! As we read of distant mission fields it is easy
to see and deplore the blight of nominal Christianity. But
let us be very careful to think first of the beam in our own eye
before we criticize. I am convinced that there is far too little
living under the Cross among our ordinary Church members.
Why is there such a truly appalling lack of leaders in almost
every parish one knows about? Why are most of the churches
making very little progress and having very little influence
upon the communities in which they are set? Would it not
be true to say that a great many of us here in England, where
it is dead easy to be a nominal Christian, have forgotten the
inevitable Cross? "I assure you," said Jesus, "that unless a
grain of wheat falls into the ground and dies, it stays all by
itself." What is that "dying" but the willing sacrifice of our
time, interest, sympathy, talents, and love, to God's Purpose?
How can we envisage the divine Purpose in merely local
terms? The whole vast holy war against ignorance, superstition, fear and disease, should surely be the concern of the
whole Church and not the anxiety of an overburdened few.
I believe that to be parochially-minded is not only stupid and
antiquated but positively suicidal. Although we do not give
either money, prayer or service primarily in order to get, but
because we love and are concerned, yet it is undeniable as
we read our Church history or even observe the churches
around us that those churches are spiritually the richest who
give the most generously.

In all the busyness of English parish life we cannot always

appreciate the appalling disparity between the crying needs of the Church overseas and the comparatively lukewarm response given by the parishes at home. Of course, I know there are magnificent exceptions, but as I have read these many moving letters and reports which C.M.S. has put at my disposal, I found myself wishing they could be made "compulsory reading" for at least all parochial church councilors. I found myself asking: "Could people read these letters, which contain not a word of conplaint, but which in their need cry out to Heaven, and still refuse to bear any part of this burden? Could people fail to be stirred by this unadvertised courage and devotion? Could they, if they knew even the simplest facts, still plead that they were 'too busy' to intercede in prayer for these soldiers of Christ? Knowing even a part of the desperate needs apparent on every hand could they still stick to their story that they are already 'giving all they can'?" I suppose some people could be as hard as that.

But most of the good people who compose our congregations here at home are not really hardhearted; they are just woefully ignorant. Their conception of missionaries and of the life of churches overseas generally is frequently at least fifty years out of date. They have often no knowledge at all of present-day situations, and unless their ignorance can be dispelled it seems to me that the split between the largely static Church at home and the necessarily dynamic Church abroad will widen yet more, and that will be to everybody's loss. The uninformed Church, inert and without vision, can only recede into the stagnant backwater of traditional Christianity.

For myself I should not hesitate to say that this sheer ignorance is, next to unthinking Cross-dodging, the reason why the Church at home fails to give anything like the proper support which the courageous front-line Church should receive. So long as the words "missionary work" conjure up in people's minds no more than a picture of a rather dull-looking missionary in a sun helmet, sitting under a palm tree, Bible in hand, addressing a crowd of respectful but abysmally ignorant "natives," no one is going to get very excited about helping. You think that an exaggeration? I assure you it is not! I know from innumerable conversations that the average member of many average churches in this country knows almost nothing of the contemporary battle with ignorance, fear, disease and evil. People simply do not know, for instance, of how the missionary with the Gospel fits into the modern pattern, which is largely that of nations emerging into self-consciousness after centuries in the "deep freeze" of a primitive ignorance. They do not know that the modern missionary may indeed have to be a specialist in any of a dozen different aspects which affect the wholeness of man. They know nothing of the work he is doing in the fields of medicine, agriculture, education, rehousing and local government. Neither do they know anything of the tensions and problems which confront Christian nationals. Because they know next to nothing their imaginations remain unfired and their hearts remain unstirred. And in the meantime the small lonely army pursues its strenuous and unadvertised way, hampered at every turn by lack of support. The handicaps of climate, language and isolation surely represent enough difficulty without the added disadvantage of feeling that the people at home, except in comparatively rare instances, neither know nor care.

It was Christ Himself who warned people that "to whom much is given of him shall much be required," and it would do us all a power of good if we in this country quietly reflected upon how much is given to us. We take for granted freedom to worship as we please, freedom from persecution, adequate doctors, nurses and hospitals, a high standard of education, probably the finest legal system in the world, an excellent police force, and a general climate of public opinion which has been influenced through the centuries by Christianity. We take it as a matter of course that cruelty to children, cruelty to animals, and bribery, for instance, should be regarded by the majority of people as evil things. Similarly, we regard it as perfectly natural that selfless service, devotion to duty, and the willingness to make sacrifices for a good cause should be universally admired. It needs a strong effort of the imagination to realize that there are scores of places where none of our Christian traditions exist and where the climate of public opinion is quite indifferent to what would fill us with horror. Yet it is into these dark places that the Light is being taken by courageous men and women who have nothing to rely upon, humanly speaking, but themselves. It is often in surrounding darkness, and under the threat of persecution, that the Young Churches are continuing to live under the Cross. Can we as Christians, who should ourselves be living under the Cross, secure in our tiny island, close our eyes, our hearts and our pockets to the needs of those who work where the battle rages hottest?

During the last few years the word "global" has come into our vocabulary in the sense of "world-wide." This is because far-sighted men in commerce and politics can see that modern facilities for travel, communication and dissemination of ideas are rapidly breaking down many of the barriers between peoples which have existed for thousands of years. The very existence of such organizations as the United Nations and its associated activities shows how, more and more, mankind is becoming conscious that all men are at least potentially brothers, and that the peoples of the world are "members one of another" whether they like it or not.

Now if the industrialists and the politicians can begin to envisage problems of industry and government on a world-wide scale, surely it is not too much to ask that every true Christian should readjust his thinking about the Church, the Universal Society founded by Christ Himself. We have no means of judging how the early disciples reacted when Christ's final command was given to them to "go into all the world and preach the Gospel to every creature." We may be sure that they could not have realized the full implication of that staggering instruction. Perhaps it is only within recent years, as the world awakens and opens up before our eyes, that we can see the extent of the commission given to the Church to which we belong. There must be far more of us who think of the Church in "global" terms. There must be an end to this absurd division between the Church "at home" and the Church "overseas." It is one Church, at any given time in different stages of development and performing different functions in different places, but it is one Church. Could that honestly be said to be the conception of the average member of the Church of England today? I seriously doubt it. He may be proud of "his" church, proud of his vicar's sermons, proud of the number of communicants, proud of the fact that his church gives so much to missions; how often do we find him proud of the fact that he is a member of a world-wide organization instituted by Christ Himself? The limited scope of the Prayer for the "Whole State of Christ's Church Militant Here in Earth" of the 1662 Prayer Book represents much more nearly the view of the average Anglican. Three hundred years ago there was some excuse for not realizing the magnitude of the task, and contemporary thought did not encourage the idea that we are "all in it together." But a great deal has happened since then, and the Anglican of today has little excuse for not knowing how the work of Christ has expanded and for not caring for his brethren who are the tiny Christian minority in pagan lands.

This book has been given the title of *The Church Under the Cross* because that part of the Church which I have tried to present is quite plainly living in such a condition. But basically and fundamentally the whole Church, and that includes every individual member of it, should be living under the Cross if it is to prove an effective instrument for God's great Purpose. It is not merely my personal conviction but the unanswerable lesson of Church history that where the Church fails to live under the Cross it fails utterly. The façade, the buildings, the ceremony, the titles, and all the other externals may remain, but if the Cross is not faithfully accepted and borne the life has departed and the Church is no more than a venerable shell of a past glory. In this country the Cross is easy to dodge. We can forget about faraway battles; we can pretend that they are nothing to do with us; we can become so immersed in the petty successes of our own parish that we never hear the cries of human anguish from the distant battlefield. But if we do this we not only fail our brethren most miserably, we not only hold back in the day of opportunity, but we condemn ourselves to a poor pale shadow of genuine Christian living. The awful price of evading the Cross is the slow death of our own souls.

But there is no need to fritter life away in the dark no-man's land that lies between the cheerful unthinking pagan and the joyful committed Christian. The way of the Cross which is offered to us by Him who died upon the Cross carries a rich satisfaction to those who accept it which is beyond the imagining of those who only peep upon it fearfully from the outside. We think of the story of Beauty and the Beast, of how Beauty, swept by tenderness and pity, at last embraced the Beast affectionately. In the twinkling of an eye the Beast was transformed and Beauty held in her arms the young Prince whom she had always loved. Is this not a parable? Do not the needs of our fellows, the ignorance, fear and evil that curse the world, repel and frighten us? Yet, if we allow Christ's love and pity to overcome our natural repugnance and fear, if, for His sake, we embrace the unlovable, is it not true that the very Beast which we loathed and feared becomes the Prince whom we have always loved?

It is acceptance which is the hard thing. The Devil and all his angels conspire to make us feel how constricted and miserable we should be if we were living under the Cross. But they are wrong, and we ought to remember that the Devil has been a liar from the beginning. The gay, unconquerable drive of the Young Church was possible only because the early Christians accepted living under the Cross without demur. Since those early days nothing fundamental has been changed by a hair's breadth. God is the same, the needs of the world are the same, and the way of victory is the same. There are no short cuts, and no alternatives—nineteen hundred years of human history have proved that. The men and women of whom I have written have grasped unhesitatingly the opportunity of cooperating with God. They have found that the way of the Cross is the way of real living, rich, satisfying and vital. They do no less than share the life of God, and at the end of their earthly road there is the certain promise of Life for all eternity. Have we at home lost our vision by overfamiliarity with what are in fact breath-taking realities? Have we allowed our sensitivity to be blunted because we are physically so safe and secure? Let us think again of the awful need which led the Young Prince of Glory to leave His Heaven and come to the rescue of mankind. Let us hear afresh His parting command to preach the Gospel to every creature. If we are blind and deaf we lay up for ourselves tears and bitter regret as Reality breaks upon us, as one day it surely will. But if we hear and see, if we dare to take the way of love which He took, we have the unspeakable joy of His companionship in all that life may bring, and the unutterable satisfaction of knowing at the last that we fought in the good fight, and have our share in the Final Victory.

266
P56